# Introduction to Psychodynamics

WITHDRAWN

*Frederick R. Hine,* M.D.

Introduction to Psychodynamics:
A Conflict-Adaptational Approach

WITHDRAWN

DUKE UNIVERSITY PRESS   DURHAM, N.C.   1971

L.C.C. card no. 71–142292 / I.S.B.N. 0–8223–0244–6

Supported in part by U.S. Public Health Service
Mental Health Training Grant MH-07435

PRINTED IN THE UNITED STATES OF AMERICA
BY KINGSPORT PRESS, INC.

# Foreword

This volume derives from a series of lectures which its author has presented to first-year medical students at Duke University Medical Center for nearly a decade. Dr. Hine has been convinced that familiarity with the field of psychodynamics constitutes one important facet of the student's knowledge of the behavioral sciences. His goal has been to distill from Freudian and neo-Freudian sources the concepts essential to the construction of a working model of certain aspects of the human psyche, and he has chosen to focus on the aspects most commonly involved in the distress and misery which cause people to seek help. The presentation centers upon the interaction of emotions within the individual and his patterns of interpersonal adaptation. Neurosis is regarded as a ubiquitous human process rather than a list of disease entities, and the effort is to demonstrate the applicability of psychodynamic principles in helping people in various kinds of distress. By eliminating all but the essential concepts it is possible for the student to begin to grasp these applications quickly and to include a dynamically grounded psychotherapeutic element in all his contacts with patients. The model is simple enough to be quickly grasped, but complete enough to be functional.

While the conflict-adaptational approach itself is a simplified distillate of psychodynamic thought, its points of articulation with more complex and more controversial aspects of psychodynamic theory and with other areas of the bio-behavioral sciences are frequently indicated. This feature, together with the suggestions for further reading, makes the volume a suitable point of departure for the student who finds that he wishes to extend his knowledge of psychodynamics or to pursue integrations with other fields.

As a lecture series and in the form of a mimeographed lecture syllabus, earlier versions of this material have been found useful by students and beginning residents in psychiatry. I believe that in its present form the usefulness of Dr. Hine's "blue book" will be continued and extended.

Ewald W. Busse, M.D.
*J. P. Gibbons Professor and Chairman*
*Department of Psychiatry*
*Duke University Medical Center*

# Contents

# Introduction

The measure of a theory is its usefulness. A theory is good insofar as it enables us to predict relationships between observed objects and events in nature. There is considerable satisfaction in being thus able to understand the natural world and in the resulting ability to control, to some degree, the events of nature. As we are able to predict natural relationships, we can, within limits, influence and control them by introducing events which have predictable effects. The medical activity of diagnosis and treatment is, of course, an example of the application of scientific theory.

While a single, coherent theoretical system encompassing all known observations would obviously be desirable, it is rarely achieved even in highly developed areas of scientific study. In the less developed sciences, multiple, overlapping theories employed side by side are typically found. The presence of these complementary points of view or "windows" through which observed data may be organized and understood, while putting a burden on the student, need not lead to discouragement if he keeps in mind that we ask of theory that it be useful, not that it be the ultimate and final truth.

As the sciences of human psychology and psychological medicine emerged in the late-nineteenth century, it became apparent that the traditional medical model of disease entities was not sufficient to provide understanding of certain types of human misery and distress. Modern psychiatrists, together with members of closely related professions, have therefore erected alongside the traditional diagnostic system of theory a structure of psychodynamic theory which they use to complement the former—shifting from one system to the other, perhaps emphasizing one more than the other with a particular patient, but never totally ignoring either one.

To complicate matters further, psychodynamic theory has itself become a complex structure of alternate, complementary points of view. Deriving in large measure from the work of Sigmund Freud, this theory reflects in its various points of view the several periods in the development of Freud's thinking. More recent developments within psychoanalysis proper, as well as the important contributions of the early dissidents, the neo-Freudian school, and the biological, behavioral, and social sciences generally, have added facets to the structure of psychodynamic theory.

The pages that follow attempt to present an introduction to psychodynamic theory sufficiently brief to allow rapid assimilation, but sufficiently complex to provide real assistance to the student in understanding his patients' verbal and other behavior and in planning his own responses. From the large body of Freudian and neo-Freudian theory these pages select for emphasis the concepts *inner conflicts* and *techniques of adaptation.* It is hoped that these concepts, as developed below, will provide (1) sufficient grasp of the essentials of psychodynamic theory to permit meaningful interaction with patients and (2) a core of theory to which more psychodynamic knowledge and knowledge from other behavioral sciences may be added by the student who wishes to develop further the psychosocial aspects of his professional competence.

Part I of the book (chapters 1 through 9) presents the conflict-adaptational approach to psychodynamics. Part II consists of supplementary chapters which deal, in a rather rudimentary fashion, with certain areas of the bio-behavioral sciences essential to a complete grasp of conflict-adaptational psychodynamics. These are heredity and constitution, conditioning and learning, and personality development, including mother-child relationships. To varying degrees this material will be familiar from undergraduate course work in psychology, sociology, anthropology, or biology. For some students the supplementary Part II will serve principally as a stimulus to memory, while for others it may be an introduction to unfamiliar areas. Whenever possible the reader is referred, at the appropriate points in Part I, to the relevant supplementary chapters.

### Reading notes

Full appreciation of psychodynamic theory comes, of course, only with the study of the original work of its creators, beginning with Sigmund Freud. His *General Introduction to Psychoanalysis* [1916–17] (New York: Liveright, 1935; paper edition, Washington Square Press) provides an excellent entree to the field. The book consists of a series of lectures given by Freud to skeptical students at the University of Vienna. It has also been translated under the title *Introductory Lectures on Psychoanalysis* in volumes 15 and 16 of James Strachey, ed., *The Standard Edition of the Complete Psychological Works of Sigmund Freud* (London: Hogarth Press, 24 vols., 1953———). This multivolume set, now complete except for the index volume, makes available all of Freud's writings on psychoanalysis, together with frequent editorial notes which provide perspective. For permission to quote passages from this edition of Freud's works, acknowledgement is due to Sigmund Freud Copyrights Ltd., the Institute of Psycho-Analysis, and the Hogarth Press Ltd. Further perspective on Freud in relation to his work is to be found in Ernest Jones, *The Life and Work of Sigmund Freud* (3 vols.; New York: Basic Books, 1953–57). The one-volume abridged edition is less satisfactory in that it emphasizes life events to the neglect of works.

Charles Brenner, *An Elementary Textbook of Psychoanalysis* (New York: International Universities Press, 1955; paper edition, Doubleday Anchor), provides a concise summary of Freud's major tenets and later developments within "orthodox" Freudian psychoanalysis. Somewhat less clearly organized but with many valuable points is Robert Waelder, *Basic Theory of Psychoanalysis* (New York: International Universities Press, 1960). Otto Fenichel, *The Psychoanalytic Theory of Neurosis* (New York: Norton, 1945), is an encyclopedic presentation of psychoanalytic thought; and Alexander Grinstein, *The Index of Psychoanalytic Writings* (New York: International Universities Press, 9 vols., 1956–1964), is useful as a source of references on specific topics.

The conflict-adaptational approach to psychodynamics derives most directly from the "adaptational psychodynamics" of Sandor Rado and from the so-called neo-Freudians, especially Harry Stack Sullivan. The basic source for the former is Sandor Rado, *Adaptational Psychodynamics: Motivation and Control* (New York: Science House, 1969). Rado's collected papers appear under the title *Psychoanalysis of Behavior* (New York: Grune & Stratton; vol. 1, 1956; vol. 2, 1962). The best approach to Sullivan and the other neo-Freudians is probably through Clara Thompson, *Psychoanalysis: Evolution and Development* (New York: Hermitage House, 1950; paper edition, Evergreen). Also useful are Ruth Munroe, *Schools of Psychoanalytic Thought* (New York: Dryden Press, 1955); chapter 4 of C. S. Hall and G. Lindzey, *Theories of Personality* (New York: Wiley, 1957); chapters 70–72 of Silvano Arieti, ed., *American Handbook of Psychiatry* (New York: Basic Books, 1959); and chapter 7 of A. M. Freedman and H. I. Kaplan, eds., *Comprehensive Textbook of Psychiatry* (Baltimore: Williams & Wilkins, 1967).

One of the specific aims of the conflict-adaptational model is to provide an approach to psychodynamics which permits ready articulation with other psychological approaches (e.g., learning theory, developmental psychology) but also with behavioral neurobiology at one end of the spectrum of behavioral sciences and sociology at the other end. The research literature in behavioral neurophysiology and neurochemistry increases so rapidly that a satisfactory integrative review is difficult to find. A collection which reveals the range of areas involved is D. C. Glass, ed., *Neurophysiology and Emotion* (New York: Rockefeller University Press, 1967). Many recent but classic studies in the neurophysiology of behavior are in R. L. Isaacson, ed., *Basic Readings in Neuropsychology* (New York: Harper & Row, 1964). A good introduction to the sociological areas relevant to psychological medicine is David Mechanic, *Medical Sociology: A Selective View* (New York: Free Press, 1968).

# Part I. Conflict-Adaptational Psychodynamics

# Chapter 1. Inner Conflicts

## I. Neurotic process

**A.** One of the major concerns of clinical psychiatry is those forms of human misery which appear to be the result of the individual's learned patterns of response. Unhappiness of this type seems to be the result neither of gross disruption of bodily function nor of insoluble external problems. What we observe, rather, is an individual with an intact body in a life situation which seems to offer reasonable opportunities either for satisfaction or for change who, by his own behavior patterns, converts each opportunity for pleasure into the largely self-inflicted misery we call neurosis.

**B.** In certain respects the specific misery-producing behavior traits themselves differ only in "intensity" from the learned traits which combine to form the normal personality. Thus general principles of learning and socialization apply with equal force to the study of neurosis, and the patterns of feeling and behavior characteristic of neurosis may be observed in varying degree in everyone. This essential continuity between normal and neurotic behavior patterns makes it possible to use one's empathy and identification with the sufferer as a means to clearer understanding of the sources of his self-defeating traits. It must not, however, be permitted to obscure recognition of neurotic traits by means of the rationalization "Everyone does that to some degree, so there can be nothing wrong."

**C.** Although the distinction is one of quantity, for practical purposes it is usually possible to distinguish neurosis from non-neurotic life adaptations. This distinction is not made merely for the purpose of labeling the patient "neurotic," but so that the contribution of neurotic processes to a particular symptom or unsatisfying life area may be evaluated and the neurotic element in most human suffering may be recognized and reduced.

**D.** The concept of inner conflict has proved a useful one around which to order observations of total personal functioning and interpersonal relations, particularly observations which bear on the question of neurosis.

## II. Inner conflict and neurosis

**A.** Our basic inference from the observations to be described next is that *the learned patterns which characteristically give rise to prolonged misery are patterns of inner conflict, of opposing motive forces (emotions), one of which is some form of learned, excessive, unrealistic fear.*

## III. Recognition of inner conflict: the recognition of neurotic process

**A.** Persistent or increasing misery which appears out of proportion to real bodily dysfunction or environmental problems raises the question of neurosis, and even in the presence of major organic or environmental disaster the physician should be alert to a possible neurotic element in a patient's unhappiness.

**B.** The presence of neurotic conflict is revealed not so much by the specific nature of the symptoms and complaints as by a fluid, dynamic triad of interrelated behavioral signs: (1) the emotions of distress, namely, anxiety and depression, (2) the inappropriate inhibition of one type of behavior, and (3) the inappropriate exaggeration of another, contrasting type.

    **1.** Excessive fear or depressive affect may be observed in the following forms:

        **a.** Excessive fear of people and other external stimuli, excessive concern over bodily illness or injury (hypochondriacal fears), phobias (displaced fears), excessive "worries," feelings of remorse, shame, and guilty fear.

        **b.** States of distress without specific external referents, such as anxiety, "nervousness," "tension," etc.; feelings of depression, "loss of interest," "emptiness," despair.

        **c.** Physiological effects of emotional (autonomic) discharge such as the moment-to-moment responses (blushing, tremor, overbreathing), the more persistent effects (nausea, headache, diarrhea, etc.), and even the structural changes of psychosomatic illness.

    **2.** Certain natural and necessary aspects of human behavior (the "instincts" or "instinctual drives" of psychoanalytic theory) are partially but distinctly and inappropriately inhibited, as reflected in the following observations:

   **a.** The behavior is rarely expressed freely even when such expression would be entirely safe and useful and even when deliberate effort is made (as in the psychiatric interview) to enable or facilitate their expression; i.e., there is "resistance" to such expression.

   **b.** The impulses reach behavioral expression only when more or less concealed within a "compromise" which emphasizes an opposite type of motivation, or in highly disguised form as (1) dreams and fantasies, (2) spontaneous denials, (3) slips of tongue or pen, or (4) inappropriate, explosive outbursts.

**3.** The overt behavior patterns of the individual — his defenses, symptoms, character traits, interpersonal characteristics, in short, his adaptive efforts — contain some expression of the blocked impulses, but reflect the relative weakness and distortion of this "instinctual" limb. The resulting "compromise" patterns are typically dominated by exaggerated and rigid *opposites* of the inhibited "instincts" (reaction formation, reactive character traits). Such inhibition-derived, reaction-dominated patterns are frequently inappropriate to the specific circumstance and to adult life generally and thus, in the long run, tend to intensify rather than relieve distress.

**C.** There is a fourth sign of neurotic conflict for which the observer should be alert: the presence of *a dynamic interaction between the first three.* Increased external or internal demand for the feared, inhibited behavior leads to increased manifest anxiety and depression unless further exaggeration of opposite patterns is possible. Heightened distress is regularly followed by efforts to intensify these reactive patterns, both in the consulting room and in other areas of the patient's life. Conversely, pressures to give up the reactive patterns lead to increased signs of distress.

### Reading notes

J. C. Nemiah, *Foundations of Psychopathology* (New York: Oxford University Press, 1961), is a valuable source for further discussion of basic psychodynamic concepts together with illustrative case examples. See particularly pp. 23–26 on dreams and fantasies as indicators of conflict, pp. 51–52, 108 on spontaneous denial, pp. 113–14 on slips of the tongue, pp. 72–73 on resistance, and pp. 120–21 on compromise formation.

# Chapter 2. Inner Conflicts: Some Theoretical Aspects

## I. The concept of conflict

**A.** "Conflict" is a central concept in most psychodynamic theories of personality and neurosis. Shortly after his original discovery that neurotic symptoms are not simply the result of trauma but are related to ideas and memories which are blocked from conscious recall and expression, Freud came to recognize that the block is part of an *active process* which is itself a part of the individual's personality. If recall of an idea proves to be impossible without special treatment it is so because the idea is unacceptable to the conscious, moral, socially oriented part of the personality, which sets up the block. Very soon thereafter Freud made the further discovery that the active inhibitory process is directed more toward wishes than toward memories per se, the wishes being thereby prevented from reaching conscious awareness or open expression. This conflict paradigm of force and counterforce, urge and inhibition, became a central tenet of psychoanalytic theory from its earliest period. Grinker discusses its historical importance:

Many other people knew about the unconscious before Freud's time. . . . But these were for the most part unsystematic presentations of hunches or intuitions and led to no operational procedures and certainly not to the development of systems of thought. No one preceding Freud could adequately relate the unconscious to motivation, direct or indirect, and its vicissitudes. It is interesting that the major emphasis which led Freud to develop a *system of concepts* was his emphasis on conflict between opposing forces. — R. R. Grinker, "A philosophical appraisal of psychoanalysis," in J. H. Masserman, ed., *Science and Psychoanalysis*, 1: 126–143, 1958. (Quoted by permission.)

**B.** In Freud's writings the concept is occasionally mentioned explicitly, both in relation to neurosis and to the more general psychoanalytic theory of personality:

Psycho-analysis, too, accepts the assumption of dissociation and the unconscious, but relates them differently to each other. Its view is a dynamic one, which traces mental life back to an interplay between forces that favor or inhibit one another. — "The psycho-analytic view of psychogenic disturbance of vision" [1910], *Standard Edition*, 11: 213.

In such people [who develop neuroses] we regularly find indications of a contention between wishful impulses or, as we are in the habit of saying, a psychical conflict. One part of the personality champions certain wishes while another part opposes them and fends them off. Without such a conflict there is no neurosis. — *Introductory Lectures on Psychoanalysis* [1916–17], *Standard Edition*, 16: 349.

The ego renounces these functions which are within its sphere [as when a patient experiences a neurotic inhibition of some function which would be desirable and useful to him] in order not to have to undertake fresh measures of repression, in order to avoid a conflict with the id. — *Inhibitions, Symptoms and Anxiety* [1926], *Standard Edition*, 20: 90.

From the very first we have said that human beings fall ill of a conflict between the claims of instinctual life and the resistance which arises within them against it. — *New Introductory Lectures on Psycho-analysis* [1933], *Standard Edition*, 22: 57.

C. The concept of conflict is implicit in all periods of Freud's writings even when not specifically mentioned. It is inherent in such pairs of antithetical forces as intolerable ideas vs. will, strangulated affect vs. repression, memories of childhood seductions vs. repression, pregenital sexual impulses vs. disgust, shame, and morality, incest wishes vs. force of repression, thoughts vs. dream censor, sex instincts vs. ego instincts, id vs. ego, instincts (sex and aggression) vs. anticathexis. This list of antitheses is a somewhat shortened version of that given by Peter Madison, *Freud's Concept of Repression and Defense* (Minneapolis: University of Minnesota Press, 1961), p. 125. In a similar vein Reuben Fine writes, "This concept of an inner conflict is an Ariadne's thread which runs through the whole history of psychoanalysis." — *Freud: A Critical Re-evaluation of His Theories* (New York: McKay, 1962) p. 12.

D. For Waelder it is just this emphasis on inner conflict which distinguishes Freudian theory from the popular view which holds that external events (problems, life stresses) are sufficient to explain neurotic illness:

With its emphasis on inner conflict as a necessary step in neurosis formation, Freudian theory stands in opposition to a trend of thought which is both ancient and new. . . . Mental illness, insanity, has since time immemorial been attributed to the impact of external events. In the early nineteenth century, the famous French psychiatrist Esquirol listed a number of factors which in his view were responsible for a mental break, e.g., loss of property, insult to one's honor, or frustrated love. In the mind of the public, mental illness is often attributed to a tragic experience or to overwork. It is tempting to see neurosis in a similar light, as a reaction to unfavorable external conditions.

This view is actually held by other psychotherapeutic schools, including representatives of the "dissident" or "liberal" schools of psychoanalysis. — Robert Waelder, *Basic Theory of Psychoanalysis* (New York: International Universities Press, 1960), p. 38.

## II. Conflict theory does not preclude other theories

**A.** "Conflict" and related intrapsychic concepts can be included in theories which also give major emphasis to adaptation and the importance of the external world. It is true, as Waelder notes, that certain of the "dissident" and neo-Freudian theories, in their determination to emphasize the whole person in his interaction with his current interpersonal-social milieu, have largely disregarded inner conflict and other intrapsychic concepts. (Adler, Fromm, and Sullivan make little or no use of the concept of conflict. Horney uses the term, but in a somewhat different sense.)

**B.** Efforts to focus attention upon the interacting, adapting, outward directed functions of the individual have been a most important but relatively more recent development in Freudian and closely related schools of thought. One element of the neo-Freudian critique has served to point up this earlier lack and what may have been at times an undue emphasis on inner processes. But it seems that the model most likely to be useful is one which includes carefully conceived concepts representing both intrapsychic and interpersonal-social events. We will call such a theoretical model *conflict-adaptational*.

1. One advantage of retaining intrapsychic concepts is implicit in the quotation from Waelder. It is obvious that two people exposed to the same external event (environmental stress) do not inevitably both react in the same way, e.g., do not both necessarily develop self-defeating neurotic behavior. There are individual differences — some innate and some learned — and there is a need for concepts to describe and summarize these differences. The reaction of a person to a given situation certainly can be better understood or predicted if, in addition to variables describing the situation, we include variables which refer to the behavioral characteristics of the person as an individual organism. (To the degree that a psychological concept is defined in terms referring specifically to the individual we may consider it "intrapsychic." Short of moving to the biological level of observation, this is about all we can mean by the word.)

2. A theory which includes intrapsychic concepts is not prevented thereby from recognizing the importance of life experience, including especially childhood experience, as well as innate capacities in the development of individual personality. Writing in the highly intrapsychic language of the Freudian structural theory (id, ego, super-ego) Fenichel remarks: "The motives of defense are rooted in external

influences. However, the external world as such cannot repress. . . .
An original conflict between the id and the external world must first
have been transformed into a conflict between the id and the ego
before a neurotic conflict can develop."—Otto Fenichel, *The Psychoanalytic Theory of Neurosis* (New York: Norton, 1945), p. 130.

3. A second very important advantage to retaining behaviorally defined, intrapsychic concepts is the increased possibility of rap-
prochement with the biological sciences. Biology, although fully
aware of the organism as an open system, deals largely with inner
processes. Insofar as progress has been made toward bridging the
psychophysiological gap in our knowledge, intrapsychic concepts,
including psychoanalytic structural and affect theories, have played
an important role.

## Reading notes

The works quoted above to document the central importance of inner conflict
in psychodynamic theory provide extended discussions of this concept. The
contributions of Rado and the discussions of Sullivan cited under Reading Notes
in the Introduction are here pertinent to the effort to integrate classical and neo-
Freudian views under the rubric "conflict-adaptational." Another very important
paper dealing with this subject from an adaptational viewpoint is Abram Kardiner
et al., "A methodological study of Freudian theory" (four parts.), *J. Nerv. Ment.
Dis.* 129: 11–19, 133–143, 207–221, 341–356, July-September 1959; reprinted,
with critical commentary and discussion in *Internat. J. Psychiat.* 2: 489–596,
September 1966. Franz Alexander is important in the line of those providing
integration of contrasting points of view. A key reference is F. Alexander, "Un-
explored areas in psychoanalytic theory and treatment," *Behav. Sci.* 3: 293–316,
October 1958. His collected papers have been published: F. Alexander, *The
Scope of Psychoanalysis, 1921–1961* (New York: Basic Books, 1961).

# Chapter 3. Fear and "Instinct": The Elements of Neurotic Conflict

## I. The theoretical concept "fear"

**A.** It is possible for higher organisms to learn to respond to a wide variety of stimuli with the somatic motor, visceral, and biochemical behavior characteristic of the innate responses to tissue damage and pain. The learning process is essentially that of classical conditioning. It has proved useful to summarize these responses in the concept of "fear" and to view fear as an internal stimulus-producing response occupying an intermediate position between external stimuli and the total behavioral response pattern of the organism (see chapter 11 below for further discussion of classical conditioning).

 1. The characteristic somatic motor responses to fear, as to pain, are broadly described as *avoidance,* i.e., efforts to escape or prevent encounter with the relevant stimuli. The visceral-biochemical changes in fear have been described and are considered to constitute the necessary metabolic background for avoidance, the "preparation for flight."

**B.** As a learned *response* it appears from experimental work that fear is rapidly learned but extinguishes with difficulty.

**C.** As a *drive stimulus* fear seems to occupy a prepotent position among the various drives simultaneously competing for expression.

 1. From the standpoint of natural selection it is not difficult to see that these characteristics of fear might have considerable survival value for a species by favoring the rapid and firm learning of danger signals and assuring that avoidance of danger will take precedence over other needs. It may well be that the development of the *ability to anticipate pain and damage* before their occurrence (this capacity is associated with the evolution of distance receptors and the neocortex) has permitted the evolution and survival of the highly complex vertebrate forms. Man, of course, is the outstanding example of the value of foresight. But man's strength is also at times his weakness: the capacity to anticipate danger, to learn fear, makes man the species most vulnerable to neurosis (see chapter 10 below).

## II. "Fear" and "anxiety": the question of definition

**A.** In an effort to point up the changing significance of fear under differing conditions, psychoanalysts and other theorists have made distinctions between the definition of "fear" and definitions given for "anxiety." At present the weight of opinion seems to favor retaining some distinction. Unfortunately, however, various writers do not always make the same distinction. To illustrate: Anxiety (in contrast to fear) is defined as a response to *unreal* danger, as a fear response to *unknown, vague,* or *unconscious* stimuli, or as a response to *internal* (rather than external) danger signals. All three of these distinctions are somewhat related to each other and to the role of fear (or anxiety) in neurosis, but they are not the same.

**B.** In order to avoid confusion and inconsistency, no attempt will be made to distinguish between "fear" and "anxiety." The two words will be used as synonyms, necessary distinctions being made by means of modifying words and phrases.

**C.** A brief study of the three distinctions between "fear" and "anxiety" will, however, reveal much about the role of fear in the neurotic conflict.

1. The fears of the neurotic process are unrealistic fears — either totally inappropriate responses to nondangerous stimuli or, more commonly, exaggerated responses to real dangers, revealing in their excesses the unrealistic element. Typically, the fears which give rise to neurosis derive from a time in the patient's life when he was both more helpless and vulnerable (and therefore in greater real danger) and less able to evaluate accurately the reality of external threats. Neurotic fears are usually outmoded (but not outgrown) responses from earlier life periods.

2. It is quite usual in neurosis for the patient not to be aware of the stimuli which give rise to his fears or of the connection between the stimuli and the response. In fact, the patient is almost never aware of the most important fear-inducing stimulus, the "instinct" itself. Repression from consciousness is usually a part of the more general process of inhibition.

3. The third distinction, that between internal and external stimuli, may refer to two related but different matters. As has been said, the internal "instinct" itself is an essential ingredient of neurosis. Without this persistent need there would be nothing to hold the individual to the problem. So the "instinct" may be the inner stimulus for fear.

In this view, we are dealing with fear as the cause of inhibition, as a cause of conflict. It is also important to recognize a *level of fear or anxiety* which is most often the result of conflict. This motive state of conflict-caused anxiety may reach levels of intensity which result in massive inhibitory or avoidance behavior (e.g., panic) and in gross, direct disruption of cortical and other bodily functions.

a. Freud's widely discussed two theories of anxiety have, as their major point of difference, emphasized fear as a cause of conflict (the later theory) and fear as a result of conflict (the earlier). In our view of the total process of neurosis, both are important.

### III. Fear as conditioned response

A. Recognizing that neurotic fear is invariably a learned response, we may ask whether the nature of the original unconditioned stimulus and learning circumstances is of importance. It would seem that the original painful circumstances giving rise to the new fear associations (the unconditioned stimulus) are retained in a general way as the *feared consequence*. In psychoanalytic theory fears (anxieties) are often classified according to the feared consequences:

1. *Separation anxiety.* Fears based on early interpersonal deprivation of the helplessly dependent infant and the resulting painful increase in various body tensions may persist as fears of desertion, rejection, loss of the love object.

   a. It is rare, in my experience, to encounter a neurosis of any severity in which fears of interpersonal loss are not central to the neurotic process. Whether this was true in Freud's day (when castration anxiety was viewed as the pervasive neurotic fear) and simply not recognized or whether there has been a real change due to changing social patterns (e.g., less use of bodily punishment) is not clear.

2. *Castration anxiety.* Fears based on bodily injury, physical punishment, or threats thereof persist as fears of damage to the body, including the genitals but by no means limited to them.

3. *Guilt (guilty fear).* If there has been an emphasis in the learning situation on verbal repetition of parental prohibitions, on using the parent as a model, on abstract ethical and moral reasons for inhibiting impulses, there may be some of the factors which predispose to a shift from "pure" fear to guilty fear. The feared parental punish-

ments (desertion, bodily damage) are said to be now internalized to form the conscience. Neither the presence of the punishing agent nor even the possibility of his future presence (parents may be dead) is any longer necessary to produce inhibition.

4. *Shame.* This is a not too well understood subvariant of fear in which the possibility of discovery by the disapproving, punitive authority seems to play a significant part.

**B.** It is important, in the treatment of neurotic patients, to make some evaluation of the feared consequence in order to avoid behavior which may suggest rejection, threats of attack, or judgmental criticism, since this will directly increase the fear response, provide circumstances for further learning of the undesired, unrealistic learned fears, and increase the anxiety level. Some suggestion of rejection or the like often cannot be avoided, of course, but the therapist can be prepared to counteract its effects through interpretation and other aspects of his behavior if he recognizes what is going on.

**C.** *Perception and cognition* are given places of central importance in some theories of personality and psychopathology. It should be clear that theories which emphasize the ways in which stimuli are interpreted, the meanings given to situations, provide an alternative way of stating what we have been saying about learned fears: the individual comes, through experience, to perceive certain situations as dangerous. At times in the therapy of some patients, interpretations within the framework of perceptual theory may be more effective than those which deal with motivational concepts.

**D.** A number of psychodynamic theories stress the importance of *self-esteem* and conception of self. Again, this would seem to be, in many ways, another side of the fear concept. In terms of self-concept, "I fear I will be rejected" may mean "I am weak and helpless," and guilty fear, of course, "I am evil." Self-esteem and intensity of fear seem to be inversely related. In therapy it is often most important to keep these relationships in mind in order to understand the patient's statements and in order to make your own statements meaningful to him.

## IV. Instinctual drive

**A.** For the purpose of discussing neurotic disorders we have reluctantly chosen to retain the term "instinct" or "instinctual drive" for the partially inhibited limb of the inner conflict. Our criteria for including a concept in the list of instinctual drives are that it must be generally present in man and continuously or periodically active. This means, in effect, innate biological drive responses "fed" by innate biological stimulus sources; or innate responses to circumstances inevitably and repeatedly encountered in human life; or a "secondary" drive universally learned as a result of the conditions of human life and deeply learned so as to remain a potent driving force. For our purposes the "instinctual" drive must be in general (though not under all conditions of relative intensities) lower in the precedence hierarchy than fear, a stipulation which arbitrarily but usefully removes from our list the drives whose gratification is necessary to support life.

1. "Instinct" is not here used in the sense of the animal biologist's term, which commonly is intended to include entire patterns of complex responses (e.g., nest building).

B. As in the case of fear, the presence of any instinctual drive is inferred from observations of behavior. The classification or subdivision of these drives is therefore dependent upon the classification of behavior, a most complex subject which has been approached in a wide variety of ways. As we move to the adaptational or "output" side of our model this problem will be discussed in more detail and the following list of instinctual drives should become more meaningful. For the present, so that we may move on, the list will be presented most briefly.

1. Sex

a. Freud initially meant genital sexuality but subsequently broadened the concept to include all pleasure strivings based on bodily satisfactions. There is no doubt that these functions generally and genital sexuality specifically are very frequently involved in conflictual processes and therefore very frequently inhibited as part of the neurotic process. While it is certainly possible for sexual function alone to be inhibited, the usual situation involves the inhibition of genital function as part of inhibition in one or more of the broader interpersonal behavior areas. Thus what is typically observed is the inhibition of sex-as-aggression, sex-as-submission, or sex-as-affiliation, or some combination of these three.

2. Aggression

a. Sex and aggression are the two "instincts" in most modern versions of Freudian theory. Aggression was originally considered a part of pregenital sexuality (sadism) but later given a more independent place. In fact, Freud's concept of "death instinct" is viewed by the many Freudians who do not employ its biological or philosophical implications as important because of its having been Freud's vehicle for giving aggression a place of independent importance.

  b. For reasons to be discussed later it is at times useful to distinguish between at least two kinds of aggression, (1) hate or rage and (2) assertiveness or domination.

3. Trust (closeness, intimacy, affiliation, love)

4. Submission (dependency)

  a. In talking about the various instinctual drives, we are referring to the natural, normal impulses to seek satisfaction and pleasure through these various modes of interpersonally directed behavior. Unfortunately both "submission" and "dependency" in our particular society tend to connote only submission and dependency of excessive, abnormal degree. It is nevertheless necessary to use the words in this list of instinctual drives because no other suitable words are available. (This is, of course, an interesting commentary on our independence-oriented society.)

*Reading notes*

Whole volumes have been written about fear and anxiety in relation to neurosis and disordered behavior. On Freud's two theories Charles Brenner, *An Elementary Textbook of Psychoanalysis* (New York: International Universities Press, 1955), pp. 76–88, is excellent. Two additional discussions are Clara Thompson, *Psychoanalysis: Evolution and Development* (New York: Hermitage House, 1950), pp. 112–30; and Rollo May, *The Meaning of Anxiety* (New York: Ronald Press, 1950), pp. 112–27. The primary sources are Freud's clinical papers from the period 1894–1900 (*Standard Edition,* vol. 3) and his *Inhibitions, Symptoms and Anxiety* [1926] (*Standard Edition,* vol. 20).

The contribution of learning theory to our understanding of fear and the neurotic process is discussed by John Dollard and N. E. Miller, *Personality and Psychotherapy* (New York: McGraw-Hill, 1950), and by Joseph Wolpe, *Psychotherapy by Reciprocal Inhibition* (Stanford, Calif.: Stanford University Press, 1958), chap. 6.

A more clinically oriented presentation of the concept of anxiety, with numerous references to the psychoanalytic and psychiatric literature, is H. P. Laughlin, *The Neuroses* (Washington: Butterworths, 1967), chap. 1.

# Chapter 4. The Vicious Spiral of Neurosis

## I. An overview of the conflict-adaptational model

**A.** You will recall earlier statements regarding the intrapsychic or inner-conflict aspect of the neurotic process, to the effect that *the learned behavior patterns which characteristically give rise to prolonged misery are patterns of inner conflict, opposing motive forces, one of which is some form of learned, excessive, unrealistic fear.* The other vector in a neurotic inner conflict is *one of the instinctual drives.* That is to say, painful interpersonal experiences, usually in early life, have caused the individual to become excessively and inappropriately fearful of one (or more) areas of his own natural impulses toward a necessary and important area of interpersonal behavior. This classically conditioned tendency whereby the natural "instincts" come to elicit fear may be activated by any circumstance, external or physiological, which tends to arouse the instinctual drive. The distress (anxiety and depressive affect) of such persistent conflict gives rise to intense and sometimes desperate efforts at behavioral resolution.

**B.** The adaptational (behavioral output) and feedback aspects may now be added in order to complete the model: *The behavior resulting from neurotic conflict—because it is preponderantly determined by unrealistic fear, predominantly unrealistic, unnecessary inhibition of gratification-seeking activity—is very likely to be maladaptive.* "Maladaptive behavior" is behavior that tends to elicit from the environment responses which result both in painful failure of need satisfaction and in direct painful punishment (rejection, retaliation, rebuff, recrimination). *The immediate, short-range effect may be to elicit from others responses which offer reassurance for the unrealistic fears, thus producing the illusion of security. But the long-term, sum-total effect is typically painful failure and reprisal.*

**C.** *Such painful feedback results in further augmentation of the inner conflictual processes described in paragraph* **A.** The instinctual need remains unfulfilled and continues to evoke fear. The conditioned fear habit is further strengthened by association with the external pain situation. The level of distress affects is directly and immediately increased by the painful feedback. *The behavioral result is further inhibition of the* *instinctual drive and further exaggeration of the fear-dominated, reactive behavior. The probability of successful adaptation is further reduced.*

1. The process of *active neurosis* just described may be viewed as a desperate, almost continuous search for reassurance in face of unrealistic fears. Clearly behavior not responsive to the real situation but dominated by unrealistic fears is not likely to be adaptive, not likely to elicit satisfaction from the real world.

**D.** The individual who acquires many strong patterns of unrealistic fear responses is quite likely to be caught in a *descending vicious neurotic spiral* of fear, maladaptive behavior, increased fear, increased maladaptation . . .

1. But how many are too many? How deeply must the patterns be learned? Clearly these questions cannot be answered simply; it depends on circumstances. In the fortunate absence of triggering circumstances, active spiraling neurosis may not occur despite a severe neurotic predisposition. And whether the process, once started, does indeed spiral downward to disaster, stabilize at a level of more or less tolerable misery, or reverse itself depends upon the quantitative relationships within a complex of individual and environmental variables, some of which are learned, some innate, and some pure chance. The individual may find a group or person whose needs dovetail with his neurotic behavior patterns in such a manner that punishment no longer increases and some satisfactions may be retained, though often at the price of remaining partially inhibited and therefore somewhat miserable. At rare times the neurotic sufferer may establish a relationship in which punitive retaliation is withheld *and* opportunity for increased "instinctual" expression is provided. This may be called a therapeutic relationship, whether provided by spouse, a friend, a family physician, or a formal psychotherapist.

## II. Fear as a necessary factor in neurotic conflict

**A.** It seems that fear is the only affect powerful enough to block, with the consistency necessary to keep the vicious neurotic spiral turning, major biological and social drives. Fenichel notes that it would appear "conceivable for a neurotic conflict to take place between two instinctual demands with contradictory aims. Certain critical facts seem to prove, for example, that homosexuality may repress heterosexuality or that

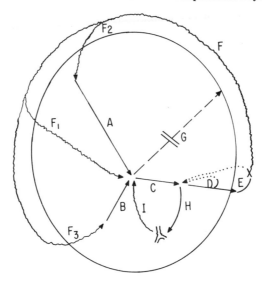

**Figure 1.** The conflict-adaptational concept of neurotic process: a diagram using vectors and feedback. Inner conflict consists of excessive, unrealistic habit patterns of *fear* (A), including guilty-fear and shame, in response to one of several instinctual drives (B), the inevitable, natural, not-to-be-completely-denied impulses toward *aggression, independence, trust,* and *submission* (which, like any stimuli, may come to evoke fear through association with painful, punitive experiences). The direct intrapersonal results of persisting conflict are: increased *distress* (C), the affects of which are *anxiety* and *depression;* efforts at distress reduction through self-deception, the classical *defense reactions* (D) centering in repression of the instinctual urges and resulting in the distress reduction known as *primary gain* (endogain). Conflict also results in interpersonal behavior (E) which, while rigidly avoiding the behavior associated with the feared instinct and emphasizing its opposite (reactive character traits), is directed toward eliciting from other people (X) distress reduction through reassurance that needs will be met without demands for the feared "instinctual" behavior. Provision of this reassurance by others is known as *support,* and its feedback effects as *secondary gain* (epigain). The individual with significant conflict(s) resulting from intense, inappropriate fears (represented by the length of vector A) of his own instinctual drives, but who is able to successfully reduce his distress by defensive and interpersonal techniques sufficient to maintain emotional equilibrium, is said to be *neurotically predisposed.* In this state instinctual needs are partially satisfied through dreams and other symbolic disguises and by disguised, partial expression imbedded in the fear-dominated reactive behavior. The individual is primed, however, by his intense fear potential for disequilibrium, the positive feedback, non-self-correcting vicious spiral of active neurosis; that is, active neurosis is likely except under circumstances of an unusually tolerant environment or one which happens to "fit" his restricted behavioral repertory.

*Active neurosis* may be precipitated by stressful events at various points in the circuit: physiologically or environmentally triggered increase in instinctual drive (B) resulting in increased fear (A); real external danger or other stress leading to increased distress; inability to continue the performance of defensive and/or reassurance-seeking interpersonal behavior because of, say, physical illness; gradual or sudden removal of support by the other persons (X), who may offer instead feedback of a painful, nonreassuring, "punitive" type (F), resulting in immediate increase of the distress ($F_1$), increase of the fear and of the fear habit ($F_2$), or persistence or increase of the unsatisfied instinctual drive ($F_3$). Blocked by his fear from adaptive modifications of behavior in the direction of instinct-motivated patterns (G) which might elicit satisfaction from others, the individual is driven by increasing fear to increasingly desperate use of the maladaptive reactive behavior (E), which results in further aggravation of the painful, disequilibrating feedback effects ($F_1$, $F_2$, $F_3$).

Still further activity of this vicious spiral may be generated in an internal *psychophysiological* circuit in which the autonomic effect (H) of intense or prolonged distress upon body tissues may result in dysfunction or partial destruction of, with consequent "pain" and further distress-inducing feedback (I).

In the diagram, dotted lines indicate distress-reducing, neurotic-gain, equilibrium-fostering, *negative feedback* effects. Wavy lines indicate distress-increasing, disequilibrium-producing, *positive feedback* effects. The interrupted line (G) indicates inhibited instinct-motivated behavior unavailable to the neurotically predisposed individual.

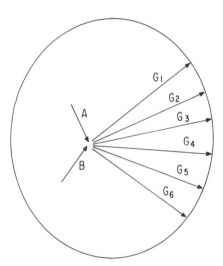

**Figure 2.** Non-neurotic behavior. In contrast with the process depicted in Fig. 1, here when fears (A) of the instinctual drive (B) are of moderate, realistic degree (and in the absence of overwhelming external stress), there is no persistent distress and a wide range of behavioral responses is available to the individual. Some of these are instinct-dominated to varying degrees ($G_1$, $G_2$, $G_3$), and some are fear-dominated ($G_4$, $G_5$, $G_6$). Flexibility to shift from one response area to another, depending upon the total current situation, is the behavioral key to freedom from neurotic predispostion and active neurosis. The non-neurotic system is set for self-correction; interpersonal failure of a particular behavior leads to its temporary inhibition and the exploration of alternative behavioral responses.

sadism may repress masochism. However, if the history of conflicts of this type is investigated it is regularly found that the apparent conflict between instincts merely covers or represents another conflict between an undesirable instinct and some fear or guilt feeling" — Otto Fenichel, *The Psychoanalytic Theory of Neurosis* (New York: Norton, 1945), pp. 129–30. Thus when it appears that a neurosis is caused by a conflict of "instincts" (e.g., assertion vs. submission) the dynamics may usefully be further analyzed in terms of two interlocking "instinct"-fear conflicts (see pp. 38–40). A conflict of two "instincts" does not produce neurosis; the myth of Buridan's ass starving in conflict between two equally desirable stacks of hay does not constitute the paradigm of neurotic conflict.

**B.** There is experimental evidence, as well as clinical, which substantiates this view. A review of conclusions derived from animal studies of conflict will serve to clarify the point. In this work it is customary to view conflict in terms of gradients of approach and avoidance response tendencies. Approach-avoidance conflicts, i.e., "instinct"-fear conflicts (in contrast to approach-approach and avoidance-avoidance) are the type which tend to produce "stable equilibrium [in which] as soon as any response gets started it produces effects which reduce its strength or increase that of its competitors. Thus, unless the first response is very strong to begin with, it is likely to lose its dominance before it is completed. The situation is like that of a ball, suspended on a string, always tending to return to a point of balance. Incompatible responses continue to inhibit each other unless there is a great difference in their relative strengths." — N. E. Miller, "Experimental studies of conflict," in J. McV. Hunt, ed., *Personality and the Behavior Disorders* (New York: Ronald Press, 1944) 1: 432. With regard to the approach-approach situation Miller writes: "Since it is extremely unlikely that the two alternatives will be perfectly balanced, and since even in such cases a slight distraction will be likely to upset the equilibrium, choices between purely desirable alternatives will be expected to be made quickly without vacillation. . . . The situation is like that in which a pencil, balanced on a razor-sharp point, starts to fall one way or the other and always topples completely over in that direction. Though incompatible, the responses do not continue to inhibit each other" (pp. 431–32, 442). Finally with respect to avoidance-avoidance situations Miller concludes: "It can be seen that as soon as the subject in a direct line between two nasty dogs starts moving to one side or the other, continuing on [at this angle away from the line] is a more direct avoidance than turning back. . . . Therefore, the situation is one of unstable equilibrium which should be easily resolved without conflict behavior. Unless hemmed in, the subject would escape" (p. 443).

### III. Depressive affect

**A.** In the preceding chapter we spoke of a level of fear or anxiety which is most often the result of conflict. Biologically this motive state is seen as providing the physiological substrate for avoidance behavior, the "preparation for flight." But increased level of fear is not the only motivational-physiological result of conflict. In almost all clinically significant conflicts the autonomic concomitants of fear are admixed with those of *depressive affect*. Just as anxiety provides both the signal that pain and loss threaten but may be avoided and the physiological energy mobilizing pathways to permit avoidance, so depressive affect may be viewed as a signal that pain is inevitable and loss already a fact and that it might be best to avoid useless expenditure of energy. The physiological concomitants of depressive affect are essentially energy-conserving. R. L. Frank has compared human depression, in its basic biological significance, to hibernation in animals.

**B.** The relative proportions of anxiety and depressive affect vary greatly with the length of time the conflict has been active, the nature of the conflicting forces, and the nature of the circumstances which precipitated the activation of the conflict. Without attempting to go into all the clinical matters usually included under the term "depression," the following points may be made.

1. The relative proportion of depressive affect seems to increase with the length of active conflict. It is as if the physiology of the organism responded to a conviction of increasing hopelessness and despaired of ever resolving the problems.

2. For reasons which are not clear, conflicts of rage vs. guilty fear seem to predispose to a particularly profound but usually self-limited type of massive depressive episode, while conflicts of trust vs. fear seem to include from the very beginning a kind of empty, hollow depressive element which may reflect the "depth" of such conflicts and the very early childhood period in which they have been laid down, as well as the intensity of the despair which they generate.

3. As might be expected, precipitating circumstances which include a distinct element of loss (e.g., loss of loved one, loss of status or position) tend to have a more significant depressive element in the clinical picture.

*Reading notes*

The excellent 1944 paper by Neal Miller to which reference is made above is strongly recommended. For more recent reviews of the experimental and theoretical aspects of conflict theory, see N. E. Miller, "Liberalization of basic S–R concepts: extensions to conflict behavior, motivation and social learning," in Sigmund Koch, ed., *Psychology: A Study of a Science,* (New York: McGraw-Hill, 1959), 2: 196–292; and I. L. Janis, G. F. Mahl, Jerome Kagen, and R. R. Holt, *Personality: Dynamics, Development, and Assessment* (New York: Harcourt, Brace & World, 1969), pp. 218–44.

The interesting paper comparing depression with hibernation is R. L. Frank, "The organized adaptive aspect of the depression-elation response," in P. H. Hoch and Joseph Zubin, eds., *Depression* (New York: Grune & Stratton, 1954), pp. 51–65. Engel has also adopted a very similar point of view with respect to the relationships between anxiety and depression. See G. L. Engel, *Psychological Development in Health and Disease* (Philadelphia: Saunders, 1962), pp. 55–56, 174–77, 382–94; and G. L. Engel, "Anxiety and depression-withdrawal: the primary affects of unpleasure," *Internat. J. Psychoanal.* 43: 89–97, March-June 1962.

# Chapter 5. Defense Mechanisms and Techniques of Adaptation

## I. The ego functions of integration and synthesis

**A.** To the extent that the individual is motivated by inner conflict (and everyone is to a considerable degree) he is trying to satisfy both his "instinctual" urges and his biologically powerful fear-motivated impulses toward safety through avoidance. The resulting behavior will reflect, of course, the need to avoid feared "instinctual" stimuli themselves and other stimulus situations associated with them. The resulting behavior will be weighted in the direction of inhibition. But seen as a whole, the behavioral result of conflict will be an attempt at *compromise,* an effort to integrate the conflicting urges and from this integration to synthesize a behavior pattern which will make possible maximum pleasure with minimum anxiety and depressive affect. Behavior patterns which produced this result in the past, especially during the malleable years of infancy and childhood, will tend to be repeated. Such patterns will have become established through instrumental (operant) conditioning (see chapter 11 below) by parents and others.

1. The basic problem described in an earlier lecture remains basic: behavior consisting predominantly of unrealistic inhibitions has little likelihood of providing a satisfying method of relating to the real world. A further complicating factor has, however, now been added to our already complex picture of the neurotic process and the forces which impel it. That factor is the specific patterns of defense and adaptation which the individual has acquired. Two men having essentially the same conflict may have learned specific "solutions" which differ in their reality effects, one tending to aggravate the spiral, the other tending to slow down the development of the neurosis.

**B.** The persistence of behavior which has the net effect of increasing pain (the "neurotic paradox") is explained as due to the ability of these learned patterns of defense and neurotic adaptation to provide immediate or rapid relief from anxiety and depressive affect. The strength of reinforcement is directly related to its temporal proximity to the conditioned response; "immediate reinforcements are more effective than delayed ones"—John Dollard and N. E. Miller, *Personality and Psychotherapy*

(New York: McGraw-Hill, 1950), p. 187. If behavior produces an immediate effect of "reassurance," it will be retained even though its delayed effects may be to elicit from the environment punishment and refusal of gratification. As we have seen earlier, it is these delayed effects which turn the vicious spiral.

1. When it is desired to focus attention on the reassurance which neurotic behavior accomplishes principally through self-deception and perceptual distortion of internal and external reality, it is customary to speak of the defensive operations of the ego (heading II below) and of the primary gain of neurosis.

2. Reference to the adaptive or interpersonal maneuvers of the ego in neurosis (heading III below) focuses attention on reassurance through partially and often temporarily successful manipulation of people in the outside world. In this connection, it is usual to refer to the fear-reducing effects as secondary gain.

## II. Mechanisms of defense: the self-deceptive aspects of neurotic behavior

**A.** It is not immediately relevant to our purposes to discuss specific defense mechanisms (reaction formation, isolation, undoing, etc.) nor to present in detail the minor additions and changes which have been made in Anna Freud's original list. Careful reading of two or three of the references on this subject mentioned under Reading Notes will provide familiarity with the various specific defenses. The medical classifications of the neuroses rely heavily upon the presence or absence of particular defense mechanisms.

**B.** *Repression* may be briefly defined as the motivated exclusion from conscious awareness of an impulse or affect as well as of its associated ideas and memories. This process of purposive distortion of awareness may, of course, be more or less inclusive of all these elements (impulse, memories, etc.) and more or less complete. The point to be made here is that it is *self-deception for the purpose of reassurance.* The central place accorded to repression by Freud and Freudian theorists, the view that the other defenses include repression or depend upon it, is, I think, a way of emphasizing the self-deceptive qualities of all "defense." Waelder writes:

Furthermore, repression seems to hold a unique place among the defense mechanisms in so far as it is present in all other mechanisms; it may occur alone or in conjunction with one of the others. In reaction formation, e.g., what happens is not only that a person becomes oversolicitous and kind to keep his aggression subdued . . . but also that the aggressive . . . impulses have become unconscious, i.e. the drive against which reaction has been formed is repressed. – Robert Waelder, *Basic Theory of Psychoanalysis* (New York: International Universities Press, 1960), p. 183.

and H. P. Laughlin:

Repression is a basic process since it necessarily precedes the operation of nearly every other mental mechanism. Many of the mental mechanisms are called into operation as reinforcements of Repression. – H. P. Laughlin, *The Neuroses in Clinical Practice* (Philadelphia: Saunders, 1956), pp. 129–30.

C. Excessive self-deception is in itself dangerous, tending to lull the individual into a mistaken sense of security and removing the problem area from the application of rational thought.

D. As noted above, the temporary reward of fear reduction through defensive self-deception is usually termed "primary gain" and is viewed as an important factor in perpetuating self-defeating neurotic defenses and the entire spiral of neurosis. In some neurotic patients reinforcement through self-deception is undoubtedly primary (i.e., of first-order importance) in maintaining specific maladaptive behavior patterns. In others the reward of extracting limited reassurance from other people (so-called "secondary gain") is of equal or greater importance. Laughlin wisely avoids the issue of primacy of importance by substituting "endo-gain" for "primary gain" and also emphasizes the essentially internal nature of this process.

E. The concept of defense places emphasis on one dimension of conflict resolution, the blocking of thoughts and feelings from awareness. In some patients this is a most important dimension; in others it seems to be a not too essential special instance of inhibition in general. In these latter cases internally focused defenses assume a position of importance secondary to the inhibition of interpersonally oriented behavior.

### III. Maladaptive interpersonal aspects of neurotic behavior

A. One implication of our emphasis on the adaptational in psychodynamics is that in all patients it is desirable to pay more attention than is paid by classical psychoanalytic theory to the following:

1. Neurotic behavior as an attempt to elicit rewarding and nonpunitive responses from others while at the same time maintaining the predominance of fear-motivated inhibition of "instinct."

2. The "secondary gain" or "epigain" (Laughlin) of temporary, partial success in this attempt to extract reassurance from others.

3. The inhibition of instinctual drives not only from awareness but also from full, interpersonal behavioral expression.

### Reading notes

Anna Freud, *The Ego and the Mechanisms of Defense* [1936] (New York: International Universities Press, 1946), is the primary source for classification and description of the various mechanisms. Descriptions of the defense mechanisms are to be found in most textbooks of psychiatry and abnormal psychology. Particularly useful are Charles Brenner, *An Elementary Textbook of Psychoanalysis* (New York: International Universities Press, 1955), pp. 87–107; L. C. Kolb, *Noyes' Modern Clinical Psychiatry,* 7th ed. (Philadelphia: Saunders, 1968), pp. 61–79; H. P. Laughlin, *The Neuroses in Clinical Practice* (Philadelphia: Saunders, 1956), pp. 72–151; Otto Fenichel, *The Psychoanalytic Theory of Neurosis* (New York: Norton, 1945), pp. 141–67; Franz Alexander, "Development of the fundamental concepts of psychoanalysis," in Franz Alexander and Helen Ross, eds., *Dynamic Psychiatry* (Chicago: University of Chicago Press, 1952), pp. 9–15.

# Chapter 6. Character Traits and Dimensions of Interpersonal Behavior

## I. Symptom and character trait

**A.** Psychodynamic understanding of neurotic illness began with the study of patients suffering from *symptom neuroses.* These were patients who presented with a symptom, i.e., some behavior pattern which the patient himself recognized and considered foreign to his personality ("ego dystonic" is the technical term). For example, there are patients with paralyzed arms, glove anesthesias, or atypical convulsive seizures (conversion hysteria), or with thoughts which constantly intrude or compelling urges which force them to perform inappropriate acts (obsessive-compulsive neurosis).

**B.** In our discussion of neurosis so far there has been no specific reference to symptoms, the emphasis being placed instead upon *behavior patterns* as compromise solutions to inner conflict. This choice has been a conscious one and reflects the view that symptomatic behavior occurs as special ego-dystonic forms of broader patterns of maladaptive behavior, that symptoms "crystallize out" of neurotic character traits. Moreover, there is no sharp line of distinction between symptoms and patterns. Patients frequently recognize as abnormal, extreme and inappropriate character traits (personality patterns) even though these traits continue to be viewed as integral parts of the personality itself (i.e., as "ego syntonic") rather than as foreign bodies. The principles which we have suggested for the understanding of the neurotic elements in character or personality traits are equally applicable to symptoms, to the classical symptom neuroses, and to the psychogenic elements in the so-called psychosomatic disorders and functional psychoses as well. With this in mind, we will continue to let the presentation revolve around the broader characterologic aspects of behavior, taking as our principal pathological focus the character neuroses or personality disorders of psychiatric nosology.

1. Parenthetically, the number of patients coming to the psychiatrist with *character neuroses* (personality disorders) is in our day much larger than the number of those whose character problems have become crystallized to include specific symptomatic manifestations.

## II. The classification of character patterns

**A.** In classifying character traits, character types, and character neuroses one may give emphasis to the intrapsychic, defensive aspects of the behavior or to its adaptational-interpersonal aspects.

**B.** In Freudian psychoanalysis there has grown up a classification system ("psychoanalytic characterology," so called) which, as you might expect, emphasizes the intrapsychic aspects. Important contributions have been made by Freud himself, Karl Abraham, Wilhelm Reich, Anna Freud, and others.

1. Some of the classification terms in psychoanalytic characterology are oral character, anal character, phallic-narcissistic character, hysterical character (or personality), obsessional character, paranoid character, masochistic character.

**C.** As you might also expect, the neo-Freudians have emphasized the outward directed, adaptational-interpersonal aspects of behavior in their attempts to classify personality types both normal and abnormal.

1. Karen Horney has described compliant, aggressive, detached, expansive, self-effacing and resigned "directions" or "trends." Erich Fromm subdivides his "orientations" into receptive, exploitative, hoarding, marketing, and productive.

**D.** Erik Erikson presents various aspects of the personality in his psychosocial developmental schema. While these do not represent personality types in any diagnostic sense, they do provide guides to certain facets of the personality which may develop normally or may be inappropriately and maladaptively exaggerated.

1. Erikson's schema (discussed in detail in chapter 12 below) points up a fact stressed by all characterological theorists: character types, normal or abnormal, do not occur in pure form, but serve as orienting concepts to areas or facets of behavior which may be maladaptively overdeveloped.

## III. Dimensions of interpersonal behavior: the "interpersonal circle"

**A.** There are no final or correct dimensions of interpersonal behavior. The theoretical system proposed by Timothy Leary and deriving in some measure from the work of Sullivan and Erikson seems to offer the advantages of internal consistency, coherence, and relative completeness. Leary's system has proved useful in a number of independent studies involving human interaction.

**B.** The concept of greatest importance for our purposes is Leary's "interpersonal circle," a systematic description of interpersonal behavior based upon two perpendicular axes, a horizontal hate-love (or disaffiliation-affiliation) axis and a vertical dominance-submission axis. On the resulting circle, interpersonal behavior may be plotted as one or another possible combination of the four factors.

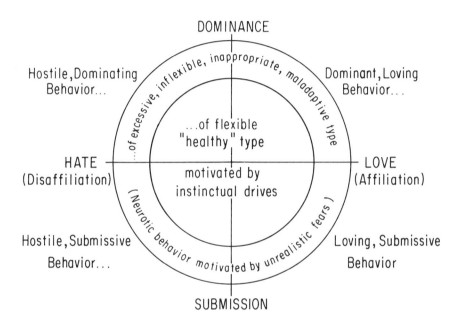

**Figure 3.** The axes of interpersonal behavior and the interpersonal circle. In adapting the interpersonal circle to conflict-adaptational theory, the outer portion of the circle (at level ı) is regarded as depicting excessive, inflexible, inappropriate (i.e., neurotic) interpersonal behavior in the various directions defined by the major axes. The inner ring of the circle (at level ı) represents the flexible (healthy) manifestations of the same range of behaviors, instinctual drive motivated behavior. Thus the behavior pattern of a non-neurotic individual at level ı might be depicted as activity in all octants in the inner ring (assuming the individual is exposed to a sufficiently wide range of environmental circumstances to make all behaviors appropriate) and no activity in the outer ring. For more detailed presentation of the particular behaviors of each quadrant, see Timothy Leary, *Interpersonal Diagnosis of Personality* (New York: Ronald Press, 1957), p. 64; or R. C. Carson, *Interaction Concepts of Personality* (Chicago: Aldine, 1969), p. 108.

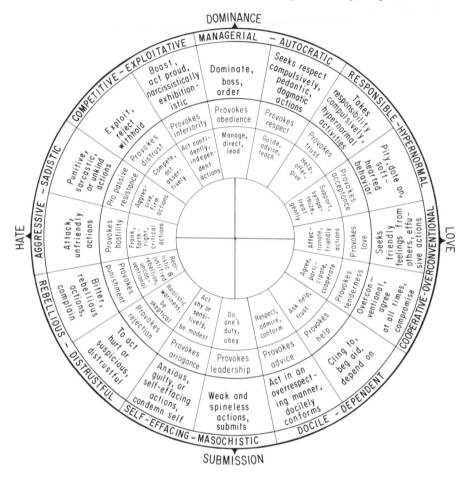

**Figure 4.** The interpersonal circle: behavioral details. Note that the more extreme, rigid, inappropriate degrees of each behavior sector are assigned to the peripheral portions of the circle. — Adapted from Timothy Leary, *Interpersonal Diagnosis of Personality: A Functional Theory and Methodology for Personality Evaluation.* Copyright © 1957, The Ronald Press Company, New York.

C. For any area of behavior, i.e., any segment of the circle, the portion nearest the center may be considered to represent the moderate employment of the particular patterns in a flexible, appropriate, and therefore adaptive way. The portion of a segment near the periphery represents excessive, exaggerated, rigid, inappropriate, maladaptive use of the same behavioral area.

D. The simplest, basic pattern of neurotic conflictual behavior is represented by excessive, rigid, inappropriate use of the overt interpersonal and overt verbal levels of behavior of segments which are opposite to the relevant "instinctual" tendencies; i.e., fear-motivated avoidance patterns are accentuated (reaction formation). At the same time the "instinctual" patterns of behavior on the other side of the circle are typically absent or inappropriately reduced at the overt levels and are apparent only in the form of partially inhibited expressions (fantasies, dreams, slips of the tongue, explosive outbursts) and are "resistant" to efforts to elicit their overt expression.

E. Another concept of importance in using the circle is that of "levels." The behavior patterns of an individual may be described at various levels: (I) overt interpersonal behavior, (II) self-description, or (III) inhibited behavior that expresses indirectly through fantasies, dreams, slips, and other disguises. A separate circular profile may be drawn for each level. The interpersonal circle and the concept of levels may be used as an aid to conceptualizing the various areas of neurotic conflict, as will be demonstrated in the next chapter.

### Reading notes

Unfortunately there are no really adequate reviews of psychoanalytic characterology. Otto Fenichel, *The Psychoanalytic Theory of Neurosis* (New York: Norton, 1945), pp. 463–540, has useful passages. J. J. Michaels, "Character structure and character disorders," in Silvano Arieti, ed., *American Handbook of Psychiatry* (New York: Basic Books, 1959) 1: 353–77, is a good source of references to the many original papers which must be consulted for an understanding of this area.

Harold Kelman, "The holistic approach," in Arieti, *American Handbook of Psychiatry*, 2: 1433–52, provides an excellent discussion of Horney's views and references to her original works. The relevant book of Erich Fromm is *Man for Himself* (New York: Rinehart, 1947). Erik Erikson's views are in his *Childhood and Society* (New York: Norton, 1950).

Timothy Leary's major work is *Interpersonal Diagnosis of Personality* (New York: Ronald Press, 1957). In addition to the theory of the interpersonal circle and the levels of personality (summarized in pp. 62–87), the student may find pp. 3–16 useful as a résumé of neo-Freudian thought as well as a discussion of its relevance to the theory of the interpersonal circle. Also excellent as a summary of Sullivanian concepts and their relation to Leary's system is R. C. Carson, *Interaction Concepts of Personality* (Chicago: Aldine, 1969), chaps. 1–4.

# Chapter 7. Areas of Conflict and Patterns of Interlocking Conflicts

## I. A classification of inner conflicts

**A.** Any system of classification, whether of "instincts," conflicts, or flowering plants, involves an arbitrary element. Classifications do not occur preformed in nature, but are imposed by the classifier. The system stands or falls depending upon its usefulness — a point to be remembered in considering the classification that follows.

**B.** An overview of the proposed classification:

1. *Aggression-fear conflicts* may include fear of both hostile and non-hostile aggressive impulses — i.e., of rage, hatred and destructiveness as well as of defiance, autonomy, independence — of sex-as-aggression, of aggressive dependency.

2. *Independence-fear conflicts* are so regularly seen clinically as an integral part of aggression-fear patterns that they are often included in that classification as suggested above. They may however occur separately.

3. *Trust-fear conflicts:* fear of trusting, closeness, intimacy, affiliation, of sex-as-affiliation, of dependency as trust and relatedness.

4. *Submission-fear conflict:* fear of submission and dependency, even though intimacy and affiliation is possible so long as the individual remains dominant. Such conflict is closely related to trust-fear patterns — perhaps a milder variant of them — but is usefully conceived as a separate area.

## II. Aggression-fear conflicts

**A.** Aggression-fear conflicts are the usual intrapsychic conflicts of psychoanalytic-psychodynamic theory — see Charles Brenner, *An Elementary Textbook of Psychoanalysis* (New York: International Universities Press, 1955), pp. 21–22, 25–32, 202. There are often important reasons for evaluating the separate contribution to the personality or the illness of conflicts over hostile or nonhostile aggression; over aggressive dependency or "oral" aggression, "anal" aggression (defiance, stubborness, rebelliousness), or aggressive, "oedipal" sexuality. All of these conflicts, however, share important common characteristics and may be usefully classified under a single heading.

**B.** The basic behavior patterns from which we infer the presence of a significant aggression-fear conflict are these:

1. Absence or relative absence (even in useful degree under safe circumstances) of direct, undisguised expressions of hostile, independent, defiant, rebellious, assertive, competitive, dominating, autonomous, rivalrous, attacking, destructive, or exploitative behavior.

    a. Under aggression-eliciting circumstances the signs of aggression will be expressed in disguised, indirect form, i.e., will be essentially restricted to level III.

    b. If the aggression-eliciting circumstances persist, either more extreme "reactive" defensive-adaptive measures (see next paragraph) will be instituted or the autonomic-behavioral indicators of distress (anxiety/depressive affect) will be increased.

2. Exaggerated, rigid, and often inappropriate use of *nonaggressive* patterns: submission, friendliness, sweetness, gay indifference, kindness, passivity, helpfulness, compliance, etc., at level I.

    a. Although nonaggression is predominant, the behavioral output reflects a compromise solution in which disguised aggression is discernible. For example, behavior which is rigidly too nice can be very punishing to those who live with it.

**C.** Patients who present with predominantly aggression-fear patterns are likely to be diagnosed as "clearly within the neurotic range" of disorder and placed in the general categories of hysterical, obsessive-compulsive, passive-dependent, depressive, anxious, phobic, or psychosomatic. On the whole, they are likely to be considered good candidates for psychotherapy (other factors, such as intelligence, ego strength, and psychological mindedness being equal).

1. Predominantly submissive behavior fits such persons well for the role of patient and arouses relatively little anxiety in the therapist (once he has acquired a basic tolerance for neurosis).

2. Other things being equal, aggression-fear conflicts tend to respond relatively promptly to application of the basic principles of psychoanalytically oriented psychotherapy.

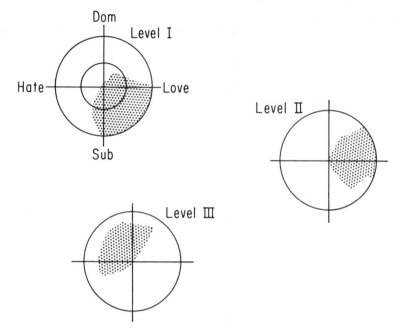

**Figure 5.** Aggression-fear conflict. At the level of overt interpersonal behavior (level I) note the absence of normal aggressive and dominant behavior (inner ring) and the presence of inappropriate affiliative and submissive behavior (outer ring). At level III note the indirect, disguised expression of aggressive and dominant behavior. The individual's self-concept and self-description (level II) may vary without changing the basic dimensions of the conflict which are represented by the level I—level III polarity. Depicted here is a self-description in which all awareness of aggression has been repressed and the individual sees himself as essentially nonaggressive, though perhaps not quite so dependent as an outside observer might rate his overt behavior.

### III. Trust-fear (affiliation-fear) conflicts

**A.** The literature of psychiatry in recent years has contained many references to problems in the areas of trust, affiliation, relatedness, and mutuality, to difficulties in a basic sense of self-esteem, to illness characterized by loneliness, detachment, and isolation. It is a major point of the conflict-adaptational approach to suggest the application of the concept of inner conflict to these problems. By conceiving of them as fearful inhibitions of trust and affiliation, it may be easier to apply many of the general dynamic-therapeutic principles to some of the patients suffering from these disorders. The concept of trust-fear conflict may also serve to differentiate these patients more clearly from the more traditionally and easily recognized types of neurosis, so that where technical modifications are required they may be more precisely applied.

**B.** The basic behavior patterns from which inner conflicts of the trust-fear type may be inferred are these:

1. The absence or relative absence (even in useful amount under safe circumstances) of free and direct expressions of love, intimacy, closeness, and trust. The sex act may be possible (often as an act of hostile domination) but there are few, if any, intimate and stable relationships.

    a. Under conditions favoring closeness, disguised and indirect behavioral expressions of intimacy and affiliation will be seen (level III).

    b. Persistence of these conditions, however, typically produces intense efforts to increase the interpersonal distance (see next paragraph) or increasing signs of intense distress or rapid alternations of the two.

2. Rigid, exaggerated, inappropriate expressions of anger, distrust, suspicion, defiance, bitterness, dissatisfaction with others, ruthlessness, exploitation, arrogance, indifference, withdrawal, detachment at level I. The predominant interpersonal effect — and its fear-motivated purpose — may be viewed as an effort to provoke rejection and increase the distance between the self and others.

    a. The attempt at compromise is evident for a time: the glimmer of hope for acceptance behind the arrogance, the yearning behind the bitter accusations. But society — our society at least — often tends to push the spiral vigorously for these people, and bizarre extremes of disaffiliation may quickly reflect intensity of panic and hopelessness, all but obscuring the "instinctual" limb of the conflict, the deep desire for closeness.

**C.** Patients who present with obvious trust-fear conflicts are likely to be diagnosed as "borderline" or "latent psychoses" and to be classified with the terms passive-aggressive, masochistic, paranoid, schizoid, narcissistic (in the more malignant of the term's various meanings), impulse-ridden, psychopathic, addicted, perverted. Often without careful study they are considered poor candidates for psychotherapy or altogether untreatable.

1. The emotional demands of such patients upon the therapist are enormous. The patient bends every effort to provoke his own re-

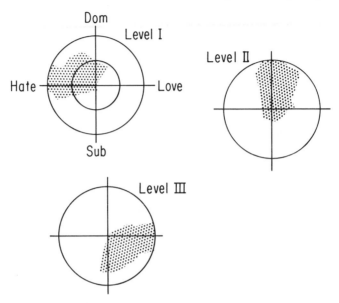

**Figure 6.** Trust-fear conflict. At level I note the absence of normal degrees of affiliative and submissive behavior. Indirect expression (level III) of these blocked strivings are observed. The subject describes himself (level II) as strong, but is unaware of the intensity of his hostile, disaffiliative interpersonal behavior.

jection, strikes at the therapist's most sensitive spots, and in his fear of closeness attempts to undermine the therapist's self-concept and capacities for human relatedness. These are the patients whose approaching therapy hour the psychiatrist anticipates with apprehension and whose departure (temporary or permanent) he may desire and unwittingly provoke.

2. We postulate that trust-fear conflicts typically have their origins in very early infancy, in a period before aggression is even possible maturationally (see Erikson's first psychosocial stage, chapter 12 below). These deep-seated, often preverbal origins of trust-fear conflicts make them less promptly responsive to the usual psychotherapeutic techniques. However, by conceptualizing the source of disaffiliative behavior patterns as trust-fear conflicts, the basic principles of psychotherapy may often be usefully applied, with appropriate modifications.

**D.** Even in patients with a presenting picture suggestive of profound trust-fear conflicts there is almost invariably a very significant aggression-fear problem as well, so that the matter of interlocking conflicts (heading V below) is intimately tied up with conflicts of the trust-fear type. An even more frequent example of this fact, perhaps, is the patient who presents with obvious aggression-fear conflicts but who, as the therapy progresses and the therapeutic relationship becomes more meaningful, begins to go sour and reveals, to the observer who is prepared to recognize them, intense problems of trust-fear.

E. The use of the word "trust" to designate this area of conflict sometimes leads to confusion and to an overuse of the concept of trust-fear conflict. There is an element of distrust involved in all conflictual processes. Any situation in which the individual consistently receives punitive, painful feedback from others is bound to result in some lack of trust. The aggression-fear-conflicted individual, we might say, comes not to trust that others will forever accept his overdependent, inappropriately nonaggressive behavior. This is a realistic fear on his part and is secondary to his primary conflict. Assuming that he has only the single aggression-fear conflict, such realistic distrust (fear of trusting) does not represent a primary trust-fear conflict as described in this section. Two points may be kept in mind to avoid this conceptual error: (*a*) primary neurotic conflicts always involve unrealistic fear, and (*b*) affiliation-fear is a synonym for trust-fear conflict.

## IV. Submission-fear (dependency-fear) conflicts

A. Just as hostile aggression and independence are often involved together in a fear-driven inhibitory process, so the instinctual-interpersonal areas of trust and submission are often bound together in a single conflictual process. Very frequently, however, normal submission and dependency may be inhibited in an individual who is able to be warmly affiliative so long as he remains in a clearly controlling, dominant position in the relationship. It is for this behavioral configuration that we reserve the terms "submission-fear" or "dependency-fear" conflict, recognizing that it is in many respects a milder variant of the trust-fear pattern probably deriving from fear-inducing experiences in a slightly later period of infancy and early childhood, the child having received sufficient reassurance in the earlier period to enable the establishment of some solid foundation of basic trust (see the discussion of Erikson in chapter 12 below).

B. The basic behavior patterns from which inner conflicts of the submission-fear type may be inferred are these:

1. The absence or relative absence (even in useful degree under safe circumstances) of free, unconstricted expression of submission,

dependency, a need to be taken care of, a turning to others and placing the self in the hands of another. Sex may be possible only under circumstances where role dominance has been clearly established.

    **a.** In circumstances where submissiveness and dependency might be useful or satisfying to the individual, these behavioral modes will be expressed in the disguised, indirect forms characteristic of level iii.

    **b.** If the submission-favoring circumstances persist, reaction-formation in the form of exaggerated patterns of dominance and independence will follow (see next paragraph) or there will be an increase in the signs of distress.

**2.** Exaggerated, rigid, inappropriate, self-defeating degrees of dominance and independent behavior, which may vary from hostile dominance to patterns of excessive benevolence and helpfulness, will be seen at level i.

    **a.** Some compromise between the "instinctual" and inhibitory limbs of the conflict is frequently seen in behavior which suggests hyperindependence and defiance (e.g., the excessive use of alcohol) but at the same time renders the individual helpless for periods of time and insures that others will in some degree take care of him.

**C.** Patients in whom submission-fear conflict problems predominate tend to be classified in both the milder and the severer ranges of functional psychopathology, reflecting the developmentally intermediate origins of these patterns.

## V. Interlocking conflicts

**A.** In chapter 4 above reference was made to Fenichel's impression that neurosis-producing conflicts which seem to involve two "instincts" are found on closer inspection to mask an underlying fear. Miller relates the persistence of conflictual behavior in apparent approach-approach situations to "latent avoidance" and "*double* approach-avoidance" conflicts. The clinical implications of this assertion are further discussed by Dollard and Miller, who write:

According to the preceding analysis, pure approach-approach choices are easily resolved; conflict should appear only when avoidance is present. This suggests that whenever unexplained indecision and con-

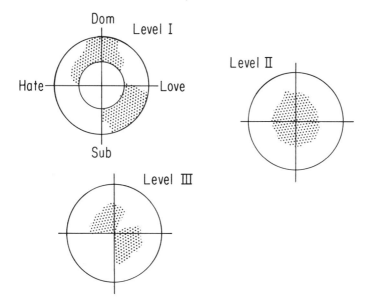

**Figure 7.** Submission-fear conflict interlocking with aggression-fear conflicts. Depicted is the typical situation in which submission-fear (or trust-fear) conflicts are overlaid with aggression-fear patterns. At level ı note the absence of *both* normal submissiveness and healthy aggression. At the same time, inappropriate, maladaptive degrees of dominant behavior alternate with inappropriate, self-defeating patterns of dependency and ingratiation. Disguised expressions of both inhibited instinctual drives are seen at level ııı. This particular individual views himself (level ıı) as essentially normal, mistaking his alternations of extreme, neurotic behavior for appropriate and useful flexibility. Once more, self-descriptions within a given conflict pattern may vary considerably.

flict appear, the therapist should look for concealed sources of avoidance. He can often profitably ask: "What is feared?"—Dollard and Miller, *Personality and Psychotherapy,* pp. 365–68.

**B.** Additional stress and anxiety may result secondarily from conflicts between incompatible neurotic behavior patterns. Clara Thompson discusses this point:

Neurotic defenses can increase anxiety in another way, according to Horney: they may be in conflict with each other. For example, early influences may lead a child to develop a great need of success and recognition. Later contacts may develop in him a contempt for [I should say "fear of"] such needs. So he remains secretly ambitious, but with a need to be modest and inconspicuous. . . . the inability to assert himself leads to his talents' failing to receive recognition. This is intolerable to his ambitious side; either anxiety must appear or a new system of defenses is added such as the presumption that he has enemies blocking his progress. Conversely, his ambition may force him to try to break his inconspicuous pose, in which case again anxiety appears or a new defense is formed. These are the people who often collapse under success and readily retreat to a dependent relationship to an authority. The pyramiding of defenses, each defense coping with anxiety, but in turn laying the ground for new anxiety, constitutes the danger from within, according to Horney. — Clara Thompson, *Psychoanalysis: Evolution and Development* (New York: Hermitage House, 1950), pp. 127–28.

C. No doubt all defenses and rigidly held adaptive techniques constitute, in this secondary sense, a burden which predisposes to further progression of the illness. Recently, however, attention has been focused in greater detail upon interlocking conflicts or "double binds." These are situations involving two specific conflicts, with two powerful fear-motivated limbs driving the individual in opposite directions. Leaving aside the specific significance for schizophrenia which has been ascribed to the fully developed theory of the double bind (i.e., the emphasis on levels of cognition and communication as well as emotional conflicts), we find a clear description of interlocking aggression-fear, trust-fear patterns and of the possible origins of such patterns:

In summary, then, we suggest that the double bind nature of the family situation of a schizophrenic results in placing the child in a position where if he responds to his mother's simulated affection her anxiety will be aroused and she will punish him (or insist, to protect herself, that *his* overtures are simulated, thus confusing him about the nature of his own messages) to defend herself from closeness with him. Thus the child is blocked off from intimate and secure associations with his mother. However, if he does not make overtures of affection, she will feel that this means she is not a loving mother and her anxiety will be aroused. Therefore, she will either punish him for withdrawing or make overtures toward the child to insist that he demonstrate that he loves her. If he then responds and shows her affection, she will not only feel endangered again, but she may resent the fact that she had to force him to respond. In either case in a relationship, the most important in his life and the model for all others, he is punished if he indicates love and affection and punished if he does not; and his escape routes from the situation, such as gaining support from others, are cut off. This is the basic nature of the double bind relationship between mother and child. — Gregory Bateson et al., "Toward a theory of schizophrenia," *Behav. Sci.* 1: 251–64, October 1956.

D. The concept of interlocking conflicts, particularly interacting patterns of trust-fear plus aggression-fear and submission-fear plus aggression-fear has wide psychodynamic importance. In actual practice the presence of double conflicts is by no means unusual. Rather than deciding which (single) conflict he is dealing with, the therapist has rather to decide which conflict area is of greater general importance in the patient's life and which is current ascendant, i.e., the more active and important in subjective experience and in determining behavior. Only by responding to the active conflict, whether with supportive or re-educative techniques (see chapter 8 below), can the therapist exert a helpful therapeutic influence.

E. It is most important that the therapist be aware of the fact that the patient's double conflict in turn puts him, the therapist, in a similar double conflict with respect to the therapeutic relationship with the patient. For example, to foster the expression of "instinct"-motivated, appropriate, moderate aggressive behavior in a patient with submission-fear as well as aggression-fear problems, without at the same time fostering disruptive, maladaptive, unrealistic fear-motivated domination and control, is a difficult task, requiring of the therapist a high degree of sensitivity and moment-to-moment flexibility.

# Chapter 8. Evaluation and Therapy: The Clinical Application of Psychodynamic Theory

## I. The conflict-adaptational model as a guide in dynamic interviewing

**A.** The relationship between patient and physician, the potential for using one's human influence for helping or for failing to help, begins immediately upon their coming together and continues on a moment-to-moment basis thereafter. The therapist should not expect of himself full and immediate grasp of all aspects of the constantly changing, multilevel communications he receives from the patient. It is necessary, however, that the therapist-interviewer have some theoretical frame of reference which will enable him to organize his thoughts concerning the patient's behavior. He must be able to respond quickly and naturally in a way that reflects his dynamic understanding and is therefore more likely to be therapeutic than ordinary social conversation. *The therapist must be constantly asking himself questions about the meanings of the patient's verbal and nonverbal behavior and finding in that behavior, as it continues to unfold, tentative answers which can serve to guide his own responses.*

**B.** Both questions and answers require words, i.e., concepts and theories, in which they may be expressed. As has been repeatedly emphasized, there are many alternative concepts and theoretical models. Each therapist-interviewer eventually finds for himself the group of concepts and relationships between them with which he can work most comfortably. His choice is based in part upon research evidence which supports the validity of concepts and postulates. But in the present state of knowledge, the choice is also based upon his own experience and his personal impressions as to which concepts have proved useful and effective in his hands. He will also, if he is wise, recognize that there are times when his favorite ways of looking at behavior fail to make clear some aspect of the patient's life. He will try to be broadly familiar with some of the many complementary ways of looking, keeping in mind that by shifting to another window he may be able to see new facets of the patient which make the whole much more comprehensible.

    **1.** Furthermore, there are not only many complementary psychodynamic-psychosocial windows which provide somewhat different

views of facets of the personality which reflect chiefly social learning. There are other windows — the formal mental examination and
formal psychological tests, the physical examination, observations
of changes in physiological functions — which reflect the influences
of heredity and constitution and of those experiential occurrences
we think of as more directly biological (infections, degenerating
diseases, etc.). Neither the psychodynamic nor the formal aspects
can be ignored in making a clinical evaluation.

C. Emphasis in this volume has been on the psychodynamic approach
to understanding the patient and, more specifically, upon what has been
termed the *conflict-adaptational* aspects of psychodynamic theory. The
therapist-interviewer who finds the conflict-adaptational model congenial
and useful will be asking himself, throughout an interview, questions
like these:

1. *Questions focused on the interpersonal adaptational aspects of
   observed behavior.* What patterns of interpersonal adaptive behavior is my patient now employing? Which areas of behavior does
   he use during the interview? Which does he report using at other
   times? Which areas seem to be unused? Which are expressed only
   partially (as in dreams, spontaneous denials, etc.)? What is he trying
   to do to me, elicit from me? How intensely does he use his favored
   areas? How rigidly does he seem to be limited to them? Can he shift
   appropriately from one area or one intensity to another as the external situation changes? Does he shift so rapidly that the stability
   and continuity of his individual personality is lost? How strongly
   does he resist opportunities and pressures to utilize the less favored
   behavioral areas? Do such pressures seem to give rise to more extreme use of favored patterns? What signs of distress (anxiety/de-
   pressive affect) accompany shifts to his less favored areas of behavior?

2. *Questions about inferred inner events.* From the answers to the
   foregoing questions what may I infer about his inner motivational
   conflicts?

## II. A conflict-adaptational conception of psychotherapy

A. This section is not a discussion of the technique of psychotherapy
but an attempt to orient the student to the process of therapy as viewed
within the framework of the conflict-adaptational model. In one sense

it may be roughly compared to a summary presentation of the anatomical-physiological principles and goals involved in a surgical procedure — information which is certainly essential but does not in itself provide the necessary technical competence to perform the operation.

**B.** Supportive psychotherapy

1. The psychotherapist accepts (within the limits of his personal tolerance) without judgment or retaliation the patient's maladaptive behavior patterns. He accepts them as at least temporarily necessary to the patient and, by refraining from imposing the usual social consequences (reprisal, rejection), attempts to interrupt the long-range feedback of pain and increasing fear which drives the neurotic spiral. This acceptance he views as a necessary first step in making possible the performance and eventual learning of behavior patterns the performance of which has in the past been fear-inhibited.

2. *This is the "supportive" element essential in all psychotherapy.* In some patients it may be all that is needed: once the spiral is interrupted (and to the degree that precipitating circumstances may have abated) the normal reward and punishment functions may enable the patient to return to his former level of functioning or even to "profit from his experience" and move to new levels of more flexible, appropriate behavior. In other instances, because of limitations in the patient, the therapist, or the situation, support may be all that is possible and may be viewed as an effort to arrest the progress of the illness or perhaps return the patient to his previous level of function but without reducing his vulnerability to future stresses. Attempts to manipulate the environment in order to minimize such stresses are often a part of the treatment.

3. While the supportive element is essential in psychotherapy, precaution must be maintained against excessive support, which may have several antitherapeutic effects. First, it can provide too much or too prolonged secondary gain, so that maladaptive patterns are reinforced. In many patients it is desirable to maintain a certain level of distress to serve as motivation for the re-educative aspect of the therapy (see below). To achieve this end, supportive activity must be "titrated" for each particular patient, using the desired level of distress reduction as the "end point." Second, the injudicious use of support may confirm the patient's unrealistic fears by communicating to the aggression-fear-conflicted patient (for example), "You are weak and helpless so I will protect you and do it for you." Excessive support for the submission-fear-conflicted

individual (and support here would take the form of permitting him to dominate the situation to some degree) might be experienced by the patient as confirmation of his fear that "you can't depend on anyone." And thirdly, support for one conflict may be nonsupportive in relation to another and coexisting conflict area. As has been noted, where there are underlying submission-fear conflicts, injudicious "supportive" encouragement of dependent behavior deriving from the more obvious aggression-fear conflict can be intensely frightening and may give rise to behavior which disrupts treatment and other areas of the patient's life (see also F. R. Hine, "Improvement of emotional support through differential diagnosis of inner conflict," *Psychosomatics* 4: 191–98, July–August 1963).

4. By providing support, by interrupting the spiral, the therapist lays the foundations for an emotionally meaningful relationship with the patient and becomes an important person to him.

C. Re-educative or personality-modifying psychotherapy

1. Within the context of his support-established relationship the therapist explores the patient's potential for a personality change through re-educative interpersonal experience. To do this he repeatedly provides opportunity for intellectual-verbal awareness ("insight") into various aspects of his inner and interpersonal life, but also, and much more important, emotional re-experiencing of them. More specifically it is hoped that the patient will challenge and come to experience the unreality of many of his learned fear responses. It should follow from this that he will sense the consequent relative safety of freer and more direct expression of the "instinct" or "instincts" involved. At the same time he may realize the needless and self-defeating characteristics of many of his reactive patterns and their failure to provide sustained satisfactions.

2. The therapist provides opportunity for the new intellectual and emotional experiences. At times he encourages and may even, through confrontation and interpretation, attempt to initiate new directions of thought and feeling when he feels the patient can tolerate such interventions without undue distress. The therapist does not, however, force or demand personality change from the patient. Actions thus evoked, based as they would be on artificially introduced, unrealistic fears, are antithetical to the basic aim of therapy, which is to free the patient and his instinctual drives from needless fear and conflict.

3. The unlearning of unrealistic fears will often result in an ability to attempt more appropriate behavior patterns, which will in turn be rewarded by the therapist himself and, hopefully, by the patient's environment outside the therapy. The success of this re-educative portion of the psychotherapeutic process thus depends not only upon the successful realignment of the patient's inner emotional forces and his freedom to try new behavior patterns but also upon certain nonconflictual matters, such as his ability to execute new and hitherto unpracticed behaviors (see chapter 9 below) and the willingness of his environment to reward and reinforce them once performed.

# Chapter 9. The Autonomous Ego Functions: Nonconflictual Contributions to Personality Formation and Function

## I. The need for the concept of ego autonomy

**A.** For any theory, efforts to apply it in research and practice bring recognition of its limitations. Thus it has gradually become clear that *there are important aspects of human activity and distress which cannot adequately be described in terms of conflict resolution alone.* Recent trends in psychoanalytic ego psychology reflect this awareness. These trends represent efforts to expand psychodynamic theory so that it may encompass additional aspects of behavior and behavioral illness and may at the same time be in closer touch with the contributions of other biological and behavioral sciences.

    **1.** The clinical importance of nonmotivational variables and points of view in problems of *organic mental disease* and *mental retardation* has never been in question. For this reason (as well as others) psychology and psychiatry have always been interested in measuring and studying such dimensions as intellectual capacity, cognition, memory, sensation, perception, and motor activity. Individual differences in the development of these functions are seen as important basic contributants to every personality, this importance being dramatically demonstrated in the organic syndromes.

    **2.** The usefulness of nonmotivational concepts in the complex problem of *schizophrenia,* while much less obvious, has remained a persistent hope. This term of Bleuler's has been used to designate a group of conditions in which the patient (who may be psychotic or less severely incapacitated) shows not only the usual behavioral signs and reduced adaptiveness of neurotic illness but also relatively fixed impairment of certain very basic mental functions, functions usually spared in "pure" neurosis. These impairments are described in Bleuler's "fundamental symptoms." Logical, coherent, purposive, thinking is disturbed. The usual connections between thought and emotional expression are weakened. The ability to integrate conflicting motives and to synthesize a consistent (even if maladaptive) pattern of behavior is partially lost. There is reduction of perceptual and attentional ties with the outer world, and often difficulty in distinguishing self from nonself. The presence of these profound disturbances has led many clinicians to argue that an adequate conceptualization of schizophrenia must include ego-weaknesses more fundamental and unyielding than those of neurosis. They feel that this is true despite the inevitable neurotic (conflict-driven) element in schizophrenic illness and despite many efforts to explain this group of disorders as simply very severe neuroses.

3. *Normal behavior* and *neurosis* itself, for which the theory was devised, also point up the need of expansion of psychodynamic theory. As one focuses more on adaptation two things become evident:

   a. The roots of many techniques of adaptation are present prior to conflict-inducing life experiences or develop as part of biological maturation, their time of emergence being relatively free of variations in conflict-inducing events (see heading II below).

   b. There are patterns of adaptive behavior which seem to arise as compromise solutions of conflict, but which persist in the personality long after the dynamic indicators of an active conflict have disappeared (see heading III below).

4. The remainder of this chapter attempts, not to deal exhaustively with the broad subject of ego psychology and ego autonomy, but merely to provide several examples to illustrate the importance of balancing psychodynamic theory with an awareness of nonconflictual contributions to behavior, personality, and psychopathology.

## II. Primary ego autonomy

A. The term "primary autonomous ego functions" has been applied to the first of these two types (3a above) of conflict-free variables. The functions or "apparatuses" of primary autonomy are those largely biologically determined anlagen which, in themselves, provide a kind of primitive adaptedness to an average environment. A partial list would include the following: sucking, grasping, eliminative, and random motor activity in the neonate; attention to moving stimuli; crawling, standing, walking; crying; the early vocalizations and the acquisition of language; acquisition of the various stages of logical thought; recall, recognition, and other aspects of memory; response to stimuli only above certain stimulus-intensity thresholds (the "stimulus-barrier"). All develop in a clearly predetermined sequence and at a more or less predictable rate, i.e., relatively independent of the presence or absence of pressures for conflict resolution. Many of these functions are, of course, promptly utilized in the processes of conflict resolution and thus become the nuclei of complex patterns of coping and defense. There is, from earliest life on, a constant interaction between the conflict-free and conflict-derived ego spheres. The personality traits which result from this interaction depend not only on the nature and intensity of conflicts but upon individual variation in the primary autonomous functions. Such variation is usually thought to be principally determined by genic or other biological influences, but life experiences such as *deprivation* of opportunity to exercise the function at a critical period may be of major importance in some (see chapters 10 and 13 below).

**B.** Schizophrenia as impairment of primary autonomous ego functions

1. Conceptualizing schizophrenic behavior as impairment of certain primary autonomous ego functions does not, in itself, reveal the etiology or etiologies of this behavior nor provide specific therapy. It may, however, help the researcher to see certain problems more clearly or the clinician to grasp relationships between his psychotherapeutic procedures and profound mental disturbances.

2. At present there is no specific therapy for schizophrenia itself. We are faced with the problem of providing treatment for patients with varying degrees of impairment of fundamental mental functions, impairments which probably have been exerting their interactive effects upon the developing personality at least since very early childhood. In our present state of knowledge such patients are treatable insofar as the therapist can relieve, by means of somatic and psychotherapeutic support, the pressures of neurotic distress upon the fragile ego and thereby prevent or interrupt the disorganizing schizophrenic psychosis.

3. Supportive therapy for the schizophrenia patient is often an incredibly complex and demanding task. The therapist must maintain his predominantly accepting, nonpunitive attitude in the face of such disconcerting phenomena as incoherent, purposeless talk, manifestly contradictory statements, lack of expected emotional responses, inattention, and misperceptions of his communications. Such fundamental impairments pervade and give a "schizophrenic flavor" to all adaptive-interpersonal behavior, which is, moreover, likely to include exaggerated trust-fear (schizoid-paranoid) patterns. Typically the schizophrenic patient has few rewarding areas of

life activity and few, if any, satisfying relationships outside of therapy. Attempts to strengthen his better ego techniques or to instigate new ones to fill in gaps that were never learned are frequently thwarted, not only by the usual fearful inhibitions of any neurosis but also by deficits in the primary autonomous functions which should serve as the core of new techniques.

4. To the degree that support is successful in averting psychosis, reeducative psychotherapy aimed at modifying neurotic conflict may be cautiously instituted, always keeping in mind that the demand for change implicit in such therapy must be carefully balanced against the danger of incapacitating disruption of ego function.

### III. Secondary ego autonomy

A. The term "secondary autonomous ego functions" (3b under heading I above) is applied to ego techniques that have been acquired because of their ability to resolve conflict and which then persist after the conflict has been reduced as a result of later experience (sometimes including the experience of psychotherapy). These patterns of behavior response, now free of their predominant fear motivation, are retained because they have proved useful in reducing other drives. That is to say, they have been rewarded. Since other drives than fear do not possess its enormous power to dominate the personality, secondary autonomous ego functions are, for the most part, an adaptational asset. The secondary autonomous ego constitutes a repertoire of relatively automatic patterns which the individual can use without conscious thought or the necessity of new learning to meet many or most ordinary life situations. At the same time they are reality-oriented (not conflict-bound or fear-bound) and may be flexibly given up as life situations change temporarily or readily abandoned if a change in circumstances is permanent. Recent writers have frequently referred to failure to develop an adequate secondary autonomous ego as a factor in emotional disorder. There appear to be at least two meanings to this concept:

1. Conflicts may persist and the individual may remain intensely fearful of his own "instincts" although there is no longer real danger to warrant such fears. In this case the ego functions in question remain predominantly conflict-driven, maladaptive excesses. This, of course, is the basic description of neurosis as we have presented it. To the degree that neurosis persists there will be less secondary autonomy.

a. It does not follow, just because exaggerations of a particular dimension (e.g., aggressive independence) which are used to resolve a submission-fear conflict are maladaptive, that all the patient's aggression and independency strivings are so motivated. Nor does it follow that therapy should be directed toward removal of all independent, assertive behavior traits. Some will prove to be responses to natural drives for independence, will have proved useful and rewarding, and will have become a valuable part of the secondary autonomous ego.

2. Another meaning of secondary autonomy as a necessary and useful development within the personality also has great importance for therapy. Functions involving behavior areas inhibited since childhood by fear will not have developed, will not have been rewarded, will not be available to the patient as more or less automatic, "natural" parts of his repertoire even when inhibitions are relieved. This point and its implications have often been overlooked by psychotherapists who seem to assume that if neurotic conflicts are modified, and inhibitions removed, the previous gaps in the spectrum of interpersonal-adaptive behavior will inevitably and automatically be filled. Paul Meehl, in an excellent paper dealing with this matter, writes:

Once we abandon the assumption that maladaptive behavior always reflects the influence of interfering forces and therefore should, so to speak, "clear up by itself" when these adverse influences are lifted by the therapeutic process, we can recognize that in addition to incompatible habits [conflicts] and disruptive affects, there are also failures to have acquired or maintained instrumental responses at sufficient strength. The therapeutic task then becomes partly one of building up such healthy responses. Of course, to attempt this while the counter-forces are still present makes no more theoretic sense in terms of the experimental psychology of learning than it does in terms of, say, classic analytic theory. I am not suggesting that we throw overboard what we know about the role of defense [i.e., maladaptive conflict resolution] in maintaining maladaptive behavior, returning to some kind of Couéism or other suggestive-suppressive therapy. I am concerned with a kind of problem which I am sure every psychotherapist . . . has met repeatedly, namely, the patient who has worked through a great deal of material, freed himself from many neurotic defenses. . . but who persists in not doing the obvious things that he himself says would now be in order, and who sometimes even raises spontaneously the mysterious question of why he doesn't get around now to doing them. This clinical problem is *not* effectively approached by searching for some yet undiscovered counter-forces. . . . Instead, we recognize that the individual's interfering habit systems have been considerably reduced by psychotherapy, but that he lacks sufficiently strong instrumental response chains of the gratification seeking type to get the behavior out and to keep it going under the reinforcement schedule of adult life. – P. E. Meehl, "Psychopathology and purpose," in P. H. Hoch and Joseph Zubin, eds., *The Future of Psychiatry* (New York: Grune & Stratton, 1962), pp. 61–69. (Quoted by permission.)

It follows that there are points in the therapy of some patients at which a more active role in reinforcing and even instigating new adaptive techniques may be desirable. It is equally true that overuse or premature use of such techniques can (as Meehl suggests) reduce psychotherapy to nothing more than the advice-giving with a pat on the back which is available (free) in almost any social setting.

**B.** While strong secondary ego autonomy is usually an asset, there are instances in which instrumental responses with great potential for self-damage become so strongly learned that they are no longer the flexible, reality-oriented techniques just described. This seems to be the case in problems of *habituation to narcotics and alcohol* and contributes greatly to the difficulties of treating these conditions. The tendency to continue drug use is notoriously resistant to psychotherapy even when there is every evidence that the source conflicts have been effectively modified. The maladaptive pattern often continues in the face of severe and obvious "punishment" from the environment. It seems likely that the tendency for drug-utilization patterns to become very strongly learned may be due to the promptness and consistency of the reward they bring, a drive-reducing, reward effect mediated by direct chemical action upon the central nervous system. Once strongly acquired, the response seems to generalize widely to a variety of emotional stimuli, so that almost any state of arousal elicits it and the "good feeling" produced by the drug may itself become a powerful and compelling secondary need or drive. Thus it is often necessary to include, in a treatment program for habituated patients, provisions for deterrent measures and for immediately available substitute satisfactions of a less self-defeating nature.

*Reading notes*

The primary source for the concept of ego autonomy is Heinz Hartmann's *Ego Psychology and the Problem of Adaptation* [1939] (New York: International Universities Press, 1958). See also Heinz Hartmann, *Essays on Ego Psychology* (New York: International Universities Press, 1964).

The best introduction to this area is David Rapaport, "The autonomy of the ego," *Bull. Menninger Clin.* 15: 113–23, May 1951. Students who find this paper of interest may wish to examine the same author's more complete exposition,

"The theory of ego autonomy: a generalization," *Bull. Menninger Clin.* 22: 13–35, January 1958.

No meaningful approach to the problems of schizophrenia can be made without first reading Bleuler's description of the fundamental symptoms: Eugen Bleuler, *Dementia Praecox or the Group of Schizophrenias* [1911] (New York: International Universities Press, 1950), pp. 1–94. For schizophrenia as a problem of ego disorder, see Leopold Bellak, "The schizophrenic syndrome: a further elaboration of the unified theory of schizophrenia," in Leopold Bellak, ed., *Schizophrenia: A Review of the Syndrome* (New York: Logos Press, 1958), pp. 3–63; Leopold Bellak, "Research on ego function patterns," in Leopold Bellak and Laurence Loeb, eds., *The Schizophrenic Syndrome* (New York: Grune & Stratton, 1969), pp. 11–65; and Leopold Bellak and Marvin Hurvich, "A systematic study of ego functions," *J. Nerv. Ment. Dis.* 148: 569–85, June 1969.

# Part II. Supplements

# Chapter 10. Evolution, Heredity, and Constitution: Significance for Psychodynamics

## I. Evolution of human nature and man's predisposition to neurosis

**A.** To the question, What phylogenetically developed characteristic makes man distinctively human? there are nearly as many answers as there are sciences which study man's accomplishments and problems. There can properly be no single, simple answer. Each new way of looking at the various products of biological evolution in man and the behavior they make possible throws new light on yet another facet of this complex organism.

1. *Man is a primate* whose erect posture and freed, grasping hands, stereoscopic vision, prolonged period of postnatal immaturity, nonseasonal female sexual receptivity, and vastly expanded neocortex *have made possible, at the behavioral level* tool making and use, a persistent need for social activity, a gathering together in families and derivative social groups, a prolonged period of sociocultural indoctrination, abstract and symbolic thought and language, enormous associative learning and memory, foresight and ability to anticipate future danger, and self-awareness.

**B.** Most important for our purpose is the fact that the massive neocortex, with its associated potential for learning subtle, abstract associations and fine discriminations of complex social cues and for anticipating danger in the absence of immediate stimuli, sits in precarious and far from complete domination atop the visceral brain and the other lower, more primitive centers. The visceral brain tends toward mass response, is capable of less discrimination, and produces effects which persist long after the stimulus is removed. These mass emotional responses exert useful but potentially dangerous effects throughout the organism. Since inhibitions are a necessary condition for life as a social being, many of the associations acquired during the period of prolonged dependency are of an inhibitory type. They are learned anticipations of pain associated with one's own needs and impulses, learned fear responses which bring into activity the mass reactions and reverberating internal feedback effects of the visceral brain. "All this makes of man an animal with a potent predisposition to the genesis of internal conflict and anxiety.

. . . Man's evolutionary endowment, successful though it has made him, contains within it hindrances to his social evolution as well as self-destructive potential."—L. Z. Freedman and Anne Roe, "Evolution and human behavior," in Anne Roe and G. G. Simpson, eds., *Behavior and Evolution* (New Haven: Yale University Press, 1958), pp. 455–79.

## II. Heredity and individual differences in behavior

**A.** None of the principal mental and emotional disorders (schizophrenia, the affective disorders, the neuroses) are directly inherited. However, there is evidence to suggest that nonexperiential factors play a role in rendering some people more vulnerable than others. Whether these predisposing factors are hereditary in the classical sense of single-gene substitutions or are the result of more complex polygenic processes is an issue very much in dispute. It is clear that such factors are rarely sufficient in themselves to produce the overt illness. (Only a few rare psychiatric diseases such as Huntington's chorea are, in this sense, directly hereditary.) Franz Kallmann, one of the foremost students and proponents of a single-gene etiological factor in schizophrenia and manic-depressive psychosis, does not suggest that "schizophrenia" and "manic-depressive psychosis" are directly inherited, but rather that an inherited "basic integrative deficiency" predisposes to schizophrenia and a "tendency to harmful extremes of emotional response" to manic-depressive disease.

**B.** The case of the mental and emotional illnesses serves to illustrate a more general and most important point. "There are no genes *for* behavior or any other phenotypic trait. Genes exert their influence on behavior through their effects at the molecular level of organization. Enzymes, hormones, and neurons may be considered as the sequence of complex path markers between the genes and a behavioral characteristic." —Irving Gottesman, "Beyond the fringe—personality and psychopathology," in D. C. Glass, ed., *Genetics* (New York: Rockefeller University Press, 1968), pp. 59–68.

1. Another statement of the same point will serve to connect this fundamental concept of behavior genetics to the schema of individual development presented in a later chapter. "But in all cases the ultimate phenotypic distinctions which we recognize as differences in personality or psychosocial response are, developmentally, many steps removed from the primary effects of the differences in genotype. Intervening between genotype and phenotype is an extensive

sequence of interactions of the developing individual with a variety of social and other environmental influences. . . . According to this concept, the genotypic constitution is but one of a large number of causal components whose dynamic interactions ultimately establish the pattern of the individual's psychosocial responses. Unless genotypic deviations from the norm are extreme [as in the case of a few rare major-gene substitutions with neuropathologic effects] we should not expect them to be in any important degree *determinative* of psychosocial phenotype."—P. R. David and L. H. Snyder, "Some interrelations between psychology and genetics," in Sigmund Koch, ed., *Psychology: A Study of a Science* (New York: McGraw-Hill, 1962), 4: 170.

2. Thus current thinking in behavior genetics emphasizes that behavior patterns are many steps removed from the individual genotype, each step consisting of an *epigenetic process of gene-environment interaction*. The concept of epigenesis is discussed in more detail in chapters 12 and 13, where it is suggested that genic recombination at the time of fertilization may be usefully viewed as a first adaptational crisis in an Eriksonian table of epigenetic development.

C. It should be clear from the foregoing that there is no point in asking the old question whether heredity or environment determines personality or a particular personality trait. Even the question of the relative contribution of heredity to a given trait is not really meaningful. The answer, often expressed as a ratio of "heritability," tells us very little about a given trait (intelligence, sociability, etc.) because of the interaction effect; i.e., the same genotype has different impact in different environments, while the same environment has different effects on individuals of different genotypes.

D. What question then can we profitably ask about heredity and behavior? In an important 1958 paper Anastasi suggested that we stop asking "how much" questions and devote attention to questions of "how" genes may give rise to particular behavior dimensions and "how" these in turn may interact with environmental variables to produce personality traits and patterns. David Rosenthal makes essentially the same point: "If we are to advance the genetics of common behavioral traits in a full and more exciting sense, we ought to get to the business of studying heredity-environment interaction. . . . To do this, we must first do three things: define the behavior of interest; delineate the genotype under study; specify the environmental variable that is coacting with it."—

David Rosenthal, "The genetics of intelligence and personality," in D. C. Glass, ed., *Genetics* (New York: Rockefeller University Press, 1968), pp. 69–78. Each of these three elements poses difficult problems, particularly for human behavior. It is instructive to look at some of the efforts which have been made to "define the behavior of interest," the dimension of behavior with which genic correlates are to be sought.

**E.** It would, of course, be very helpful in studying the interaction of heredity and environment if it were possible to work with the behavioral dimensions least removed from their genetic-biologic substrate. In addition to armchair speculation on the "basic" dimensions of human personality, the search for these simpler, more elemental psychological variables has taken a number of directions:

1. Mathematical methods are used to determine the psychological dimensions which are most nearly "unitary" in the sense of being independent of, uncorrelated with other psychological dimensions. Opinions vary regarding the validity of calling such dimensions "source traits" and considering them more basic in human personality.

2. Attempts are made to discern and verify the relationship of behavior traits with certain physical characteristics, most often body build or "somatotype." It is then assumed that traits so related to presumably inherited physical characteristics are themselves basic or "constitutional" psychological variables. This line of thought can be traced back to Hippocrates.

   a. Although clinical implications are few, psychiatrists have for several generations dutifully learned Kretschmer's pyknic, athletic, and asthenic body types and the presumed association between the first and the cycloid personality, the third and the schizoid personality. The more complex somatotyping schema of Sheldon has also aroused a continuing interest among psychiatrists, but little more.

   b. The work of Hans Eysenck combines both mathematical and somatotyping approaches, and he has arrived at conclusions which seem compatible with, rather than antithetical to, the framework of modern dynamic psychiatry. Very briefly, Eysenck's dimension "extraversion-introversion" is not only factor-analytically pure and related closely to certain very sophisticated measures of body constitution but is also found to be correlated with EEG and related physiological measures and with psychological measures of weak vs. strong conditionability. That is, extraverts are poorly able to learn associations, including learned inhibitions, while introverts are more likely to overlearn. Another basic factor, "neuroticism," appears closely related to "inherited autonomic [visceral brain] overactivity." That individuals may vary on a constitutional or hereditary basis in their susceptibility to the learning of fear responses in no way vitiates the importance of the concepts described in the earlier chapters of this book, Eysenck's antipathy for psychoanalysis and psychodynamics notwithstanding. The same is true of the possibility that individuals may vary in their tendency toward "overactivity" of autonomic-emotional responses once triggered.

3. Another approach involves the study of individual differences in behavior which are present at birth and in very early infancy, which develop at some biologically fixed time, or which manifest as relatively fixed, inflexible deficits in behavior (see chapter 13). The implication is that any one of these characteristics makes it more likely that the dimension will correlate more closely with some genotypic variable than would dimensions of a more transient nature occurring postnatally without apparent relationship to biological maturation. Clearly a number of questionable assumptions are involved in this line of thought, but it has nevertheless occupied considerable attention.

   a. As this approach involves interest in infancy and early childhood, together with biological maturation, it is very much in the Freudian tradition. Freud's own concept of the important constitutional variable seems to have been in terms of variations in the intensity of instinctual drives. One trend in modern psychoanalytic ego psychology however, has tended to place increasing emphasis upon the relatively nonconflictual (the primary autonomous ego functions, chapter 9) sources of behavior. Within this orientation, psychiatric and psychoanalytic workers have studied in infants such traits as motility ("congenital activity type"), perception (constitutional variations in the "stimulus barrier"), and synthesis or integration.

F. In the paper cited above Rosenthal also proposes (pp. 74–75) some techniques for "delineating the genotype," a difficult problem for human research since breeding and strain differentiation are not feasible. Finally, he lists (pp. 75–76) some of the environmental variables whose interaction with genotype-behavior dimension variables he thinks it worthwhile to study. Heading his list are the variables of conditioning and learning to which a central position has been given in the discussion of psychodynamic processes and which will be reviewed in some detail in chapter 11.

### Reading notes

Recommended discussions of the evolution of human nature are in Weston La Barre, *The Human Animal* (Chicago: University of Chicago Press, 1954); A. I. Hallowell, "Self, society, and culture in phylogenetic perspective," in Sol Tax, ed., *Evolution After Darwin* (Chicago: University of Chicago Press, 1960), 2: 309–71; S. L. Washburn and Virginia Avis, "Evolution of human behavior," in Roe and Simpson, *Behavior and Evolution*, pp. 421–36; and Theodosius Dobzhansky, *Mankind Evolving* (New Haven: Yale University Press, 1962). Dobzhansky (pp. 335–42) also discusses the matter of man's predisposition to emotional disorder.

The concept of a visceral brain is from Paul MacLean, "Psychosomatic disease and the 'visceral brain': recent developments bearing on the Papez theory of emotion," *Psychosom. Med.* 11: 338–53, November-December 1949.

On the genetics of mental disease and of behavior and personality in general, see Anne Anastasi, "Heredity, environment and the question 'how?' " *Psychol. Bull.* 65: 197–207, July 1958; Franz Kallmann, "The genetics of mental illness," in Arieti, *American Handbook of Psychiatry*, 1: 175–96. Dobzhansky, *Mankind Evolving*, pp. 119–24; J. D. Benjamin, "The innate and the experiential in child development," in H. W. Brosin, ed., *Lectures on Experimental Psychiatry* (Pittsburgh: University of Pittsburgh Press, 1961), pp. 19–42; J. L. Fuller and W. R. Thompson, *Behavior Genetics* (New York: Wiley, 1960); and W. R. Thompson, "Genetics and personality," in Edward Norbeck et al., eds., *The Study of Personality* (New York: Holt, Rinehart and Winston, 1968), pp. 161–74.

C. S. Hall and Gardner Lindzey, *Theories of Personality* 2d. ed. (New York: Wiley, 1970), pp. 338–79 present a discussion of the constitutional psychologies of Kretschmer and Sheldon, together with references to the original sources. On pp. 378–419 Hall and Lindzey discuss factor analytic approaches to personality. For a more detailed discussion of the work of Eysenck and his group see Hans Eysenck, ed., *Handbook of Abnormal Psychology: An Experimental Approach* (New York: Basic Books, 1961).

A valuable recent work summarizing and presenting child studies on autonomous ego functions is Sibylle Escalona, *The Roots of Individuality* (Chicago: Aldine, 1968), especially chap. 2, "Dimensions of infant behavior."

# Chapter 11. Principles of Learning and Psychodynamic Theory

## I. Learning, learning theory, and human personality

**A.** To a very large extent the behavior patterns which distinguish one personality from another are acquired through life experience, i.e., are learned. A grasp of certain basic principles of the learning process is necessary if the influence of experience upon behavior is to be understood. These principles derive largely from animal experimentation and constitute the fundamental concepts of the field of psychology known as "learning theory." While it is necessary to keep constantly in mind the more complex brain and the more complex milieu of the human organism, there is reason to believe that for purposes of understanding certain aspects of behavior these principles are valid for man as well as for other animals.

**B.** A definition of learning, taken from Kimble, will serve to highlight several important points: "Learning is a relatively permanent change in behavior potential which occurs as a result of reinforced practice."

1. The phrase *relatively permanent change* distinguishes learning from behavioral changes due to motivational changes (e.g., increased hunger), sensory adaptation, or fatigue.

2. The inclusion of *practice* (experience, training) as a necessary condition eliminates behavioral changes due to maturation, disease, or other physiological variables.

3. The characterization of learning as behavior *potential* points up the difference between learning and performance and the fact that a subject who has acquired the behavior potential may be deterred from or impaired in performing the behavior by various short-term factors—lack of motivation, inappropriate circumstances, an intervening motor paralysis, etc.

4. Practice alone does not increase the likelihood that a given stimulus situation will evoke a particular behavioral response. In fact, practice in itself diminishes this likelihood, a process known as extinction. In order for a particular stimulus-response connection to be strengthened, in order for learning to take place, *reinforcement* is

also necessary; i.e., certain additional circumstances must accompany the presentation of the stimulus and the performance of the response. The nature of these reinforcing circumstances and their relation to the S–R connection to be learned will be discussed below in connection with the two major types of learning — classical conditioning and instrumental conditioning.

## II. Classical conditioning

**A.** Classical conditioning is exemplified in the well-known experiment in which Pavlov trained a dog which originally salivated (UCR) only to food placed in the mouth (UCS) to salivate (CR) to the sound of a tone (CS) presented shortly before or simultaneously with the food. In another example, a sheep is trained to respond to a previously neutral stimulus (metronome) with hyperventilation and decreased skin resistance by pairing the metronome with an electric shock which initially evoked these responses (responses, it may be noted, usually considered indicative of emotional arousal).

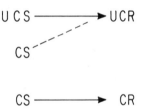

**Figure 8.** Classical conditioning. Pairing of the conditioned stimulus with the unconditioned stimulus results, after some trials, in the evocation, by the condition stimulus alone, of essentially the same response, now called the conditioned response (see the text).

**B.** In classical conditioning the reinforcing circumstance is the occurrence of the unconditioned stimulus in close temporal relationship to the stimulus to be conditioned.

**C.** For the most part the classical conditioning paradigm describes a learning process in which the learned stimulus (CS) may be any stimulating signal or situation, but the response (UCR, CR) is typically one of several primitive, relatively stereotyped patterns of glandular secretion and/or smooth-muscle contraction in viscera and blood vessels. The motor supply to these end organs is provided by the autonomic nervous system (a.n.s.) and its most intimately related "higher" centers, the hypothalamus and the limbic lobe or "visceral brain." These pathways and nuclei, remarkably similar in all mammals, are directly concerned with primitive, intraorganismic survival functions of the animal, with the mobilization of metabolic energy or its conservation, with establishing and regulating the several rather stereotyped metabolic and emotional background states of the body, states in which the much more varied, flexible response patterns of the skeletal muscular system may be performed in more direct relation to the varied demands of the external world.

**D.** Thus classical conditioning (autonomic conditioning) describes the process by which some flexibility is introduced into the body's visceral, vascular, glandular, and biochemical responses. It is the means *by which, through life experience, external events come to have metabolic-motivational-emotional meaning.* For example, fear responses, originally elicited only by some damaging or near-damaging stimulation of body tissue, can be conditioned to any stimulus in the world, which stimulus then acquires the enormous metabolic-motivational-emotional power of fear. It is important to consider two aspects of this power—the dynamic and the psychophysiologic (or psychosomatic).

1. *The dynamic aspect.* Subjectively experienced as emotions (affects), the central and peripheral autonomic responses under discussion here have the dynamic significance of motive forces (drives, urges, needs, etc.) influencing and in large measure determining the direction of externally directed motor behavior (techniques of adaptation, coping efforts), behavior mediated primarily by the somatic motor pathways and the skeletal muscles. All of the vector forces of the conflict-adaptational model have their neural substrate in such central and a.n.s. processes, and many are learned (conditioned) forces, including the learned fears so central to neurosis. The vital importance of classically conditioned fear in conflict with other drives is illustrated in the work of Masserman and others in producing experimental neuroses in laboratory animals. Obviously no human life is as simple as the highly controlled lab situation. Clinical experience suggests that a number of the basic principles apply in both animal and human neurosis, however.

2. *The psychophysiologic aspect.* Persistent states of anxiety (the result as well as the cause of neurotic conflict) involve persistent activity in the limbic and hypothalamic systems and the autonomic outflow. One result may be the stimulation of end organs to excessive or unduly prolonged activity, with consequent disruption of the internal body homeostasis and/or structural changes in the organs or other body tissues. These disruptions and lesions constitute the so-called psychophysiologic reactions or psychosomatic diseases. The psychophysiologic effects of persistent depressive affect are also of major clinical importance.

### III. Instrumental conditioning

**A.** In an experiment typical of *instrumental conditioning* (operant conditioning) a hungry cat is placed in a box equipped so that depressing a lever releases a pellet of food. After some ineffective responses the cat depresses the lever, receives and eats the food, and with repeated trials soon learns to depress the lever whenever in the box and hungry. This is instrumental conditioning of the *reward type*. In so-called *avoidance training* the experimental animal may learn to press the lever to open the door and escape from a cage in which it is subjected to painful electric shocks delivered through a grid floor.

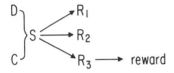

**Figure 9.** Instrumental conditioning. In a stimulus situation consisting of drives (D) and other stimuli or cues (C) the rewarded response will tend to be the one elicited by the same stimulus conditions on future trials (see the text).

**B.** In instrumental conditioning the reinforcing circumstance is *dependent upon the performance of the proper response*. This reinforcement consists of (1) some pleasure-producing stimulus or "reward" or (2) avoidance of or escape from some painful stimulus or "punishment."

   1. One important determinant of the success of instrumental conditioning is the length of time elapsing between the performance of the response and the reinforcement. The longer the delay, the less effective the reinforcement. This *gradient of reinforcement* principle is of considerable importance in understanding the acquisition and maintenance of neurotic response patterns.

**C.** If classical conditioning describes the process by which previously neutral stimuli acquire emotional meaning and motivational significance, then instrumental conditioning describes the process whereby techniques are acquired for dealing with the world in need-satisfying (motivation-reducing) ways. Thus instrumental conditioning, the "recording" of the success or failure of particular response patterns, is a major factor in the selection of specific defenses, coping techniques, and patterns of interpersonal behavior. It should not be overlooked, however, that the learning of motivations (classical conditioning) is an equally important and essential part of this process. The specifics of behavior do not depend solely upon rewards for particular responses, since the direction of behavior and the range of available responses depend principally upon the relative strengths of the drives pushing for reduction.

## IV. Relation of classical and instrumental conditioning

**A.** Although extremely useful in studying the acquisition of meanings vs. the acquisition of methods—the "involuntary" vs. the "voluntary" aspects of behavior—the distinction between classical and instrumental conditioning is an oversimplification if taken to mean that only one or the other takes place in a given circumstance. For example, in the instrumental-conditioning situation there is inevitably an element of classical: the circumstances surrounding reward or punishment come themselves to have secondary reward or punishment meaning—the box and other associated stimuli are sought or avoided and can be used (independently of the original reward or punishment) to condition other instrumental responses. Similarly, in the natural state (in contrast to the laboratory) motor behavior follows classical conditioning and instrumental conditioning occurs as the environment rewards or punishes.

**B.** The recent work of N. E. Miller and others demonstrating that autonomic responses such as heart rate and blood pressure may be instrumentally conditioned and perhaps "voluntarily" controlled may have major significance for our understanding and treatment of psychosomatic disorders. The finding that instrumental conditioning may include responses mediated by the a.n.s. contradicts the notion that the a.n.s. is exclusively an involuntary mass-reactor mediating only gross emotional responses. This finding does not interfere, however, with the validity and usefulness of the distinction between the learning of emotional significance through temporal association and the acquisition of preferred adaptive techniques through reward and punishment experiences.

## V. Stimulus generalization and discrimination

**A.** In both types of conditioning, responses learned to one stimulus will also occur when similar stimuli are presented, the strength or probability of occurrence of the response being dependent upon the degree of similarity. This tendency, called *primary stimulus generalization,* is of obvious adaptive value, since stimulus conditions are rarely exactly the same in real life.

1. Equally clear, however, are the limitations in the adaptive value of stimulus generalization. Having been bitten by a white dog, it is of obvious value to the child to fear that particular dog, may be of some value to react with caution to all dogs, is of doubtful value to be uncomfortable around all animals, and is clearly maladaptive to be uneasy with any white object of dog size. Under favorable circumstances, of course, any initial fear responses to nonharmful stimuli would extinguish as the result of exposure to those stimuli without accompanying reinforcement. This process, termed *stimulus discrimination,* describes the process by which overgeneralizations are corrected.

## VI. Stimulus-producing responses and higher mental processes

A. Not all stimuli are from outside the organism (e.g., the drive component of the instrumental training situation) nor are all responses motor acts with direct effect upon the external surroundings (e.g., the emotional-motivational responses of classical conditioning). Moreover, the two examples given are in many instances the same event: an emotional *response* which has as its chief function the *stimulation* of further behavior.

B. In addition to the motivational importance of stimulus-producing responses, learning theorists have attempted to understand the "higher" mental processes as intricate chains or networks in which language responses and their stimulus functions play the major role.

### Reading notes

For the student unfamiliar with the basic concepts of learning, G. A. Kimble and Norman Garmezy, *Principles of General Psychology,* 2d ed. (New York: Ronald Press, 1963), chaps. 6–8, is recommended. For more detailed information on animal experimentation and learning theory, consult G. A. Kimble, *Hilgard and Marquis' Conditioning and Learning,* 2d ed. (New York: Appleton-Century-Crofts, 1961).

The best presentation of the relationship between learning principles, human personality, and neurosis is John Dollard and N. E. Miller, *Personality and Psychotherapy* (New York: McGraw-Hill, 1950). The topics of generalization-discrimination and stimulus-producing responses, which have been dealt with in this chapter only very briefly, are lucidly discussed by Dollard and Miller on pp. 51–54 and pp. 97–105 respectively.

Louis Breger and J. L. McGaugh, "Critique and reformulation of 'learning-theory' approaches to psychotherapy and neurosis," *Psychol. Bull.* 63: 338–58, May 1965, provides an interesting statement of objections to this approach. A rejoinder is offered by S. Rachman and H. J. Eysenck, "Reply to a 'critique and reformulation' of behavior therapy," *Psychol. Bull.* 65: 165–69, March 1966.

The experimental neurosis work is described in J. H. Masserman, *Principles of Dynamic Psychiatry*, 2d ed. (Philadelphia: Saunders, 1961), pp. 134–35. An excellent review of the literature on experimental neurosis is P. L. Broadhurst, "Abnormal animal behavior," in Hans Eysenck, ed., *Handbook of Abnormal Psychology* (New York: Basic Books, 1961), pp. 726–63.

The body of literature on psychophysiology is very large. A good introduction to the experimental and neurophysiological aspects is P. D. MacLean, "Psychosomatics," in J. Field, H. W. Magoun, and V. E. Hall, eds., *Handbook of Physiology: Neurophysiology* (Washington: American Physiological Society, 1960), 3: 1723–44. A more detailed review of the experimental literature is J. V. Brady, "Psychophysiology of emotional behavior," in A. J. Bachrach, ed., *Experimental Foundations of Clinical Psychology* (New York: Basic Books, 1962), pp. 343–85.

References to the instrumental conditioning of autonomic responses are N. E. Miller, "Learning of visceral and glandular responses," *Science* 163: 434–45, 31 January 1969; and L. V. Di Cara, "Learning in the autonomic nervous system," *Scientific American* 222: 30–39, January 1970.

# Chapter 12. Development of the Personality: Freudian, Neo-Freudian, and Eriksonian Concepts

## I. The developmental point of view in psychodynamics

**A.** For some workers a psychodynamic formulation consists of explanations of current behavior patterns or symptoms in terms of the individual's patterns of early-life experience and relationships. That is to say, the developmental point of view is often given a place of first importance in psychodynamic theory, and possibly in psychotherapeutic practice as well. In the opinion of the present writer this is an unsatisfactory position.

1. To be sure it is intellectually satisfying to feel that one understands the "historical" origins of behavior patterns. At times it is very important to trace these origins with the patient as one way of helping him to challenge the reality of his long-standing fears and to re-experience otherwise blocked emotions and impulses. In treating patients, particularly children, it is obviously useful to know the typical problems and crises for a given age period. Certainly any preventive programs deriving from psychodynamic knowledge must include valid concept of origins. There is no question that psychodynamic theory needs its developmental or "genetic" facet.

2. Overemphasis upon infancy and childhood and upon tracing origins, however, frequently leads to needless feelings of frustration (since reliable historical data on subtle issues such as emotions and relationships are very hard to obtain in the face of the tendency to retrospective distortion). Such overemphasis also leads to needless postponement of dealing with clear and apparent current maladaptive behavior patterns on the assumption that they are not yet truly understood. Overemphasis on long-past events as causal rather than current emotional forces may foster an attitude of hopelessness or encourage interminable meandering through childhood as a way of avoiding the therapeutically necessary movement toward previously inhibited behavior areas.

3. The placement of this chapter among the supplements reflects the author's view that developmental concepts are necessary to a theory of psychodynamics, but are best viewed as supplemental

to concepts dealing with current emotional forces and behavior patterns.

**B.** The theories of development relevant to psychodynamics derive to some degree from Sigmund Freud's efforts to find important common elements among the many changes taking place in the growing infant and child. As a physician and neurologist, Freud not surprisingly chose to focus on concepts of biological maturation, the unfolding potentials of the central nervous system. But because of his interest in patients suffering from conditions which seemed to have meaning only in terms of the individual's past life experiences, Freud emphasized those characteristics of c.n.s. maturation which appeared most susceptible to influence and distortion through interaction with life happenings and circumstances. A quotation from his 1916–17 lectures will illustrate the importance he attached to this *biological-experiential interaction.*

I take the opportunity here of warning you against taking sides in a quite unnecessary dispute. . . . Are neuroses *exogenous* or *endogenous* illnesses? Are they the inevitable result of a particular constitution or the product of certain detrimental (traumatic) experiences in life? More particularly, are they brought about by fixation of the libido (and the other features of the sexual constitution) or by the pressure of frustration? This dilemma seems to me no more sensible on the whole than another than I might put to you: does a baby come about through being begotten by its father or conceived by its mother? Both determinants are equally indispensable, as you will justly reply. In the matter of the causation of the neuroses the relation, if not precisely the same, is very similar. As regards their causation, instances of neurotic illness fall into a series within which the two factors — sexual constitution and experience, or if you prefer it, the fixation of the libido and frustration — are represented in such a manner that if there is more of the one there is less of the other. At one end of the series are the extreme cases of which you could say with conviction: these people, in consequence of the singular development of their libido, would have fallen ill in any case, whatever they had experienced and however carefully their lives have been sheltered. At the other end there are the cases, as to which, on the contrary, you would have had to judge they would certainly have escaped falling ill if their lives had not brought them into this or that situation. In the cases lying within the series a greater or lesser amount of predisposition in the sexual constitution is combined with a lesser or greater amount of detrimental experience in their lives. Their sexual constitution would not have led them into a neurosis if they had not had these experiences, and the experiences would not have had a traumatic effect on them if their libido had been otherwise disposed. In this series I can perhaps allow a certain preponderance in significance to the predisposing factors; but even that admission depends on how far you choose to extend the frontiers of neurotic illness. I propose, Gentlemen, that we should name a series of this kind a "complemental series." — Sigmund Freud, *Introductory Lectures on Psycho-Analysis, Standard Edition,* 16: 346–47.

**C.** The psychoneurotic symptoms which Freud observed in his patients were such symptoms as paralyses, anesthesias, or seizures without organic basis (hysterical conversions), unrealistic fears, as of streets or horses (phobias), compelling urges to wash the hands or perform ritualistic acts (compulsions), continuous preoccupation with troubling, unwanted thoughts (obsessions), states of intense anxiety, and conditions of fatigue and weakness without physical disease (neurasthenia). As he observed and listened to his patients, these symptoms seemed most understandable as distorted expressions of certain emotional forces, forces common to all human beings but in these patients deflected from their natural course by certain kinds of early life experience. In his developmental theories, therefore, Freud stressed the biological development of the emotional forces (drives, motives, needs, "instincts") which were liable to deflection and distortion.

**D.** Freud recognized early in his work that the vital drives (for oxygen, food, elimination, etc.) cannot be blocked for long without producing death. The differences between people which result in the presence or absence of neurosis must, therefore, be due to differences in the courses taken by the nonvital drives. The first of these which came to his attention was the drive toward genital sexuality, inhibition of which seemed related to neurotic illness. Shortly after 1900, however, he came to recognize that drives toward genital activity were not the only nonvital impulses toward bodily pleasure. In certain of the perversions other parts of the body were clearly involved in "sexual" activity, and in children one can observe a sequence of pleasurable interest in these same body parts. These are patterns of repeated stimulation of the mouth (thumb-sucking) and of the anus and finally the genitals, patterns which serve no utilitarian function. Might these pleasure-seeking tendencies involving various body areas not legitimately be termed "sexual" and the corresponding body areas "erogenous zones"? By this time Freud was accumulating more observations on the symptoms, dreams, associations, and childhood memories of a wide variety of neurotic conditions. He was led thereby to broaden the concept of "sexual" to include other nonutilitarian pleasure-seeking activities involving bodily satisfaction. Some types of neurotic symptoms, it now appeared, could be more clearly understood as substitutes for blocked impulses toward nongenital bodily pleasure. For example, patients with obsessional neurosis seemed to find in their illness an outlet for aggressive ("sadistic") impulses of a sort closely associated with the tendencies toward mastery and cruelty observed in children during that childhood period when their interest is focused on anal satisfactions.

E. Freud concluded that in its biological development the sexual instinct (the psychic energy of which he termed "libido") goes through several regular stages. In each its chief route of expression involves a different part of the body. Thus, from among the many possible ways of dividing up the developmental process, Freud's biological background and his interest in neurosis led him to define the well-known oral, anal, and phallic stages of childhood psychosexual development.

## II. The Freudian stages

A. First oral (oral sucking) stage

1. The first oral stage is typical of roughly the first 8 months of life.

2. The behavioral mode is predominantly passive, receptive, dependent. Relationships with others are impersonal or only dimly personal, and involvement in the world of human beings is periodic, brief, and tentative.

3. Classical psychoanalytic theory does not emphasize the particular personality consequences of variations in life experience during this first oral period as contrasted with the second. Recent opinion suggests that it is probably the most crucial stage of development and that failure of the environment to provide adequate responses to the infant's needs to relate, depend, and receive have profoundly disruptive effects upon later personality (see chapter 13).

B. Second oral (oral biting, oral-sadistic) stage

1. The second oral stage characterizes infant life roughly from 6 months to $1\frac{1}{2}$ years.

2. The behavioral mode at this stage is demanding, aggressive seeking of satisfaction and comfort—a need to possess, with rage and envy when this need is frustrated.

3. The oral character or oral personality of psychoanalytic theory, particularly in its pathological extremes (character neurosis), is probably the result of problems arising in relation to a just awakening oral aggressiveness. Such personalities are said to be characterized by a passive-dependent, receptive orientation to life, dependent on others for self-esteem, with a corresponding desperate need for love or "narcissistic supplies." At the same time they show

a tendency to harsh self-criticism, expressing their demanding, clinging, coercive behavior only in disguised ways. Depression and manic-depressive conditions, addiction, and the impulse neuroses are the emotional illnesses to which oral characters are considered to be predisposed.

**C.** Anal (anal-sadistic) stage

1. This stage characterizes life roughly from 1 to 3 years of age.

2. Behavioral modes are typical of a period offering the first opportunity for power, independence, autonomy, and self-determination — defiance, effective hostility, productiveness, and possessiveness.

3. Some theorists have differentiated an earlier "anal expulsive" from a later "anal retentive" stage, but there is considerable doubt whether these two functions predominate in any sequential manner. More important, there seem to be few important personality consequences brought to light by this distinction between two anal stages.

4. The anal character, unquestionably the best known and most clearly described, is classically known by the triad of parsimony, obstinacy, and orderliness. He is extremely proper and pedantic, but prone to vacillation and indecision. Obsessive-compulsive and paranoid illnesses are thought to be related to abnormal anal traits. It is significant that depressions are not infrequent.

**D.** Phallic (oedipal) stage

1. This stage is represented by years 3 to 6, roughly.

2. The behavioral mode is marked by rivalry and competitive aggression.

3. This is the period of the oedipus complex. In its simplest form this complex is the hostile, rivalrous desire to eliminate the parent of the same sex and replace him in a sensual relationship with the parent of the opposite sex.

4. No very useful or widely adopted concept of a "phallic character" has been proposed. Hysterical personality traits such as suggestibility and tendencies to avoid and deny unpleasant reality, as well as hysteria itself, have for many years been linked with problems of the phallic phase. Recent findings have cast doubt on this as-

sumption. Similarly, it was for a long time held that all neuroses had their deepest roots in a failure of proper resolution of the oedipal problem, but more recently increased attention has been given to other areas of conflict, particularly those arising in the prephallic (pregenital) stages.

E. Latency

1. This period derives its name from the notion that during the grammar-school period, roughly 6 years to puberty, the sexual instincts are largely inhibited by the socializing forces exerted during the preceding oedipal phase. It is now recognized, however, that later childhood is not nearly so latent as was thought. Genital activity, for example, is not given up completely, nor is this period totally without significance for later personality development.

F. Genital stage

1. The term "genital stage" is applied essentially to postpubertal and adult maturity.

III. Fixation and regression

A. Freud used these concepts chiefly to relate psychopathology in later life to the childhood developmental stages. A quotation will illustrate:

You have heard that the libidinal function goes through a lengthy development before it can, in what is described as the normal manner, be enlisted in the service of reproduction. I should now like to bring to your attention the significance of this fact in the causation of neuroses. We are, I think, in agreement with the theories of general pathology in assuming that a development of this kind involves two dangers—first, of *inhibition,* and secondly, of *regression.* That is to say, in view of the general tendency of biological processes to variation, it is bound to be the case that not every preparatory phase will be passed through with equal success and completely superseded: portions of the function will be permanently held back at these early stages, and the total picture of development will be qualified by some amount of developmental inhibition. Let us look for some analogies to these processes in other fields of knowledge. When, as often happened at early periods of human history, a whole people left their place of domicile and sought a new one, we may be certain that the whole of them did not arrive at the new location. Apart from other losses, it must regularly have happened that small groups or bands of the migrants halted on the way and settled at these stopping-places while the main body went further. . . . we propose to describe the lagging behind of a part trend at an earlier stage as a *fixation.* . . .

The second danger in a development by stages of this sort lies in the fact that the portions which have proceeded further may also easily return retrogressively to one of these earlier stages—what we describe as a *regression*. The trend will find itself led into a regression of this kind if the exercise of its function—that is, the attainment of its aim of satisfaction—is met, in its later or more highly developed form, by powerful external obstacles. It is plausible to suppose that fixation and regression are not independent of each other. The stronger the fixations on its path of development, the more readily will the function evade external difficulties by regressing to the fixations—the more incapable, therefore, does the developed function turn out to be of resisting external obstacles in its course. Consider that, if a people which is in movement has left strong detachments behind at the stopping-places on its migration, it is likely that the more advanced parties will be inclined to retreat to these stopping-places if they have been defeated or have come up against a superior enemy. But they will also be in the greater danger of being defeated the more of their number they have left behind on their migration. —Sigmund Freud, *Introductory Lectures on Psycho-Analysis, Standard Edition*, 16: 339–41.

**B.** Several important precautions should be observed in using the concepts of fixation and regression.

1. It is tempting to adopt the view, implicit in much of Freud's writing on this subject, that overindulgence or "spoiling" at one of the early developmental stages is the primary cause of personality weakness when difficulties are encountered in later life. The accumulation of clinical experience since Freud and the available research, however, favor the view that, *rather than "spoiling," excessive deprivation and punishment—the instillation of excessive fear and guilty fear—in early life are at the core of neurotic illness.* Once that conflictual core has been installed and the basis established for relative unresponsiveness to normal feedback mechanisms, then overindulgence may play a part by reinforcing particular defenses and coping techniques, some of which may further aggravate the maladaptation.

2. Franz Alexander has correctly said, "Regression to a fixation point is a complex phenomenon, not a simple return to an abandoned developmental phase."—Franz Alexander, *Psychoanalysis and Psychotherapy* (New York: Norton, 1956), p. 104. Each developmental phase itself is a complex matter in which at least four aspects of psychic activity must be considered: (1) the needs or drives characteristic of the period; (2) the responses of the environment, often including certain typical punishments or threats of punishment; (3) the characteristic inner conflicts which develop out of the interaction between need-driven behavior and the responses of

those around the child; (4) the behavior patterns (ego defenses) eventually settled upon as the best available resolution of the conflicts. To say flatly that an individual is fixated at or has regressed to a given stage suggests that in all these aspects of his psychic life he shows predominantly the activity characteristic of that stage. This is rarely, if ever, the case. Recognition of this complexity by psychoanalytic theorists has led to the conception of various forms of regression: "instinctual" or "libidinal" regression, "ego regression," "defensive regression," "problem-solving regression." It is not essential that these particular terms be employed. *It is most important, however, to avoid the confusion which results from the oversimplified use of the regression concept. This may be done by specifying in what respect the patient's activity resembles that of an earlier life period.*

3. Not all regression is pathological, although there is a tendency to use the term as if all were. The concept "regression in the service of the ego" has been devised for a process of partial return to a childlike commune with one's own impulses, wishes and fantasies which may be a necessary part of creativity.

4. Not all psychopathology is regression. Early conflicts may employ behavior techniques characteristic of *later* periods, but in an inappropriate, maladaptive way, as when a submission-fear-conflicted patient adopts a pattern of inflexible hypermaturity as a way of insuring against being submissive. Position along the chronological-developmental continuum is not the critical criterion for psychopathology, but rather the inappropriateness, maladaptiveness of the behavior and the degree to which it fails to provide satisfaction and happiness for the individual.

## IV. Neo-Freudian influence in psychodynamics and developmental theory

A. In essence the neo-Freudian position is based upon two closely related criticisms of classical Freudian theory.

1. The neo-Freudians assert that Freud, following his discovery of his own "momentous error" (namely, that his hysterical and obsessional patients often had not really experienced the infantile sexual traumas which he had considered the cause of these illnesses), was led to make a most unfortunate shift away from concern with life experience and thereafter focused his interest almost exclusively on organic constitution.

2. The neo-Freudians argue that clinical experience fails to confirm the Freudian view that sex and aggression are the only drives of importance in neurosis. They contend that inhibition and distortion of such forces as tenderness, love, intimacy, and submission are, if anything, more commonly the sources of emotional illness than are problems of aggression or sex, even if the term "sex" is used in its broader meaning. (This second aspect of the neo-Freudian critique is met in conflict-adaptational theory by the addition of the submission-fear and trust-fear areas of conflict. It will not be further discussed in this chapter.)

B. That Freud ever went so far as to ignore the influence of life experience upon the personality is very doubtful. It is true that in one period of his life (ca. 1900–1923) his theoretical writings reflect an almost exclusive preoccupation with the inner, "instinctual" life. In the hands of his more orthodox successors, especially in Europe, the resulting *libido theory* has been employed to picture man as the outward manifestation of inner energies worming their predestined, tortuous, conflicting channels inside the individual without regard for outside events. The neo-Freudian development has served as a necessary counterbalance to such theoretical excesses.

C. With respect to the development of the individual, neo-Freudian theory defines its stages and describes their significance in terms which clearly direct attention to the impact of the world of other people. Note this emphasis upon interpersonal experience in the following brief synopsis of development as viewed by H. S. Sullivan.

1. The first stage, *infancy*, is described principally in terms of the amount and quality of preverbal, empathic communication between infant and mother. It is said to end with the development of a new method of interpersonal communication, primitive speech. Next, *childhood* is viewed as extending from the onset of ability to utter articulate sounds to the appearance of the need for playmates of one's own status at about age 5. During this period the major interaction is with parents and is of significance as the means by which the culture's requirements are indoctrinated. The early school years, called the *juvenile era*, provide relationships with peers and outside authority figures (e.g., teachers), experiences necessary for acquiring the capacity for cooperation, competition, and compromise. The very important period of *preadolescence* is marked by the development of a need for an intimate relationship with a chum of one's own age and sex. In Sullivan's opinion this relationship is

the first worthy of the name love, since for the first time the satisfactions and security of the loved one are as important as one's own. "Such a relationship entails many hours spent together in discussing all aspects of life without fear of rebuff or humiliation. One begins to see the world through the eyes of someone who is like oneself and permits the appraisal of one's own values and ideals."—Leon Salzman, *Developments in Psychoanalysis* (New York: Grune & Stratton, 1962), p. 116. The later capacity for intimacy is very much dependent upon events in this stage. *Adolescence* begins not so much with physiological puberty as with the shift of interpersonal interest from the chum to a person of the opposite sex. Dependent upon the success of relationships in this period are such personality factors as the eventual integration of lust and intimacy, the achievement of emotional and economic independence.

2. Sullivan does not ignore the biological needs characteristic of each period nor the behavioral capacities which become available in each by virtue of biological maturation. But each biological need and its related body zone is of importance to psychiatry only insofar as it creates demands for interaction with other people. If this interaction is marked by anxiety in or disapproval from the significant other, anxiety is generated in the developing child and the developing behavioral capacities are molded primarily to effect anxiety reduction rather than to fulfill needs. The result of such anxiety-induced behavior patterns is a constricted, handicapped personality. Neurosis is the result of anxiety, and anxiety is for Sullivan a strictly interpersonal event.

3. A further point should be clear from the above outline of Sullivanian stages: neo-Freudian developmental theory does not consider that all important personality characteristics have been determined by the end of the oedipal period.

## V. Ego psychology and individual development: the theories of Erik Erikson

A. Within Freudian psychoanalysis (and partly as a reaction to the neo-Freudian theories, which are also "ego psychologies") there has in recent years grown up a point of view which places major emphasis on personality functions by which the individual resolves the conflicts of maturing inner needs vs. the demands of external reality. These personality functions, which include the originally described *mechanisms of defense*, are now more broadly conceived as *coping mechanisms, adaptive behaviors*, or *ego techniques*. We will confine our interests to the principal ego psychological theory of individual development, the psychosocial theory of Erik Erikson.

**B.** Without abandoning the Freudian emphasis on biological maturation, Erikson has proposed a theory of development which seems at the same time to meet the first of the neo-Freudian criticisms.

1. In this theory the biological concepts which define the stages are broadened so that less emphasis is placed upon specific anatomical zones and more upon the characteristic behavioral mode. Thus "oral stage" becomes *oral-sensory stage, incorporation* becomes the chief behavioral mode, and *receiving, accepting*, and later *taking* become the principal social modalities. Similarly "anal" becomes *anal-muscular*, with *retention-elimination* the major behavioral modes, corresponding to *holding on* and *letting go* in the social sense. The "phallic stage" becomes the *locomotor-genital stage, intrusion* becomes its typical mode of behavior, and *making* (in the sense of taking possession of) becomes the basic social modality. (See Fig. 10).

   a. Freud's earlier work clearly anticipates and lays the basis for this theoretical development. In that work Freud relates "orality" and "incorporation," "anality" and "mastery." In Erikson's theory these insights are given new importance.

2. The developmental stages are now viewed as a biologically determined sequence of *potentialities for significant interaction with the environment*. In a sequence, and at a pace largely determined by inner laws, each of the several behavioral modes has its period of ascendancy. The significance of each period lies in how successfully its mode is integrated into the developing totality of ego functions, how successfully each phase-specific crisis is solved, how successfully a balance is achieved between the two possible extremes (e.g., naive trust and total mistrust). The establishment of each function as a useful part of later personality functioning depends in large part upon the quality of the interaction with the environment at each of these critical times. The individual is predisposed to neurotic illness by failure of those around him to provide a setting in which use of each function can develop in a manner appropriate to the larger society in which he will spend his later

| | | 1 | 2 | 3 | 4 | 5 | 6 | 7 | 8 |
|---|---|---|---|---|---|---|---|---|---|
| VIII | MATURITY | | | | | | | | Ego Integrity vs Despair |
| VII | ADULTHOOD | | | | | | | Generativity vs Stagnation | |
| VI | YOUNG ADULTHOOD | | | | | | Intimacy vs Isolation | | |
| V | PUBERTY AND ADOLESCENCE | | | | | Identity vs Role Confusion | | | |
| IV | LATENCY | | | | Industry vs Inferiority | | | | |
| III | LOCOMOTOR-GENITAL | | | Initiative vs Guilt | | | | | |
| II | MUSCULAR-ANAL | | Autonomy vs Shame Doubt | | | | | | |
| I | ORAL – SENSORY | Basic Trust vs Mistrust | | | | | | | |

**Figure 10.** Erikson's eight ages of man. Reproduced from Erik H. Erikson, *Childhood and Society,* 2d ed. Copyright © 1963, W. W. Norton & Company, Inc.

life. Typically this failure takes the form of inculcating excessive fear in one of its many forms (mistrust, shame, guilt, etc.).

   **a.** At each stage interaction with the environment is necessary for the proper development of the characteristic behavioral function. This is in some contrast with earlier psychoanalytic theory, which tended to see socialization as a preponderantly negative process, from the individual's point of view.

  **3.** The Eriksonian schema provides an epigenetic picture of development in which the dependence of later stages upon earlier is most clearly seen. It is a "building upon" rather than a "traveling over" model of development which points up the fact that the function which fails to develop at its time of ascendancy is not only impaired itself but endangers the satisfactory resolution of subsequent crises, their related functions, and the whole hierarchy of later development. Thus solution of the trust-mistrust crisis has specific significance for the subsequent behavior functions of trust, intimacy, relatedness, affiliation, etc., and also for the crises still to come, e.g., autonomy and initiative, and for the subsequent course of these functions. (Note that autonomy and initiative are aspects of aggression and independence, terms used in the conflict-adaptational psychodynamic model.)

## Reading notes

The primary sources for Freud's developmental theories are Sigmund Freud, *Three Essays on Sexuality* [1905], *Standard Edition,* 7: 125–243, and *Introductory Lectures on Psycho-Analysis* [1916–17], *Standard Edition,* vols. 15–16, especially lectures 20–22. Three papers by one of Freud's students are also classics in this field: Karl Abraham, "Contributions to the theory of the anal character [1921]," "The influence of oral erotism on character-formation [1924]," and "A short study of the development of the libido, viewed in the light of mental disorders [1924]," all in *Selected Papers of Karl Abraham, M.D.* (New York: Basic Books, 1953), pp. 370–92, 393–406, 418–501.

The secondary sources on Freudian and neo-Freudian theory cited in the Reading Notes for the Introduction contain sections on development. In addition, see Leon Salzman, *Developments in Psychoanalysis* (New York: Grune & Stratton, 1962), chap. 5. This volume also contains important statements on the second element of the neo-Freudian critique (see especially pp. 213–19). The best discussion of the first element is probably Clara Thompson, *Psychoanalysis: Evolution and Development* (New York: Hermitage House, 1950), pp. 18–58.

The primary reference on Harry Stack Sullivan's developmental theory is his *The Interpersonal Theory of Psychiatry* (New York: Norton, 1953).

Erikson's stages and concepts of epigenesis are described in detail in Erik Erikson, *Childhood and Society,* 2d ed. (New York: Norton, 1963), pp. 48–108, 247–74; Erik Erikson, "Growth and crises of the healthy personality," *Psychological Issues.* vol. 1, monogr. 1, 1959.

# Chapter 13. Development of the Personality: The "Early Deprivation" Issue

## I. Interpersonal trauma vs. stimulus deprivation

**A.** Interpersonal trauma results in fear, conflict, and inhibition; stimulus deprivation results in behavioral deficit. These two major patterns of cause and effect seem to emerge from the body of research and clinical experience involving disruptions of the usual patterns of very early life experience. These patterns in humans (and other mammals) are predominantly channeled through the mother-infant relationship, whatever may be their broader origins in family, community, societal, or international disturbances.

1. When early interpersonal experiences involve painful frustration of efforts to satisfy compelling instinctual drives (i.e., when the infant's relationships with others prove emotionally traumatic, in the psychoanalytic sense of that term), there seem to result patterns of inhibition both of the emotional expression of those instinctual drives and of the related interpersonal behavior. Along with this inhibition there are observed the signs of distress and the exaggeration of contrasting, opposite interpersonal patterns. Clearly, we are describing an early interpersonal conflict which may, if severe and prolonged, become a sufficently patterned element of the personality to warrant the term intrapsychic or inner conflict. The relevant instinctual drives involved at this early age (from six months or slightly earlier until some time into the second year of life) are those of trust, affiliation, submission, and dependency. The most frequent source of the fear-inducing trauma is the partial or total loss, from whatever cause, of the mother or a substitute mothering figure to which the infant has by this time become attached if his biological endowment and immediate postnatal period were essentially normal. The crisis lies within Erikson's trust-vs.-mistrust area; the later characterologic effects, if any, will manifest as interpersonal behavior reflecting trust-fear, submission-fear conflicts. At this early age and subsequently the inhibition of trust and the related patterns in the dynamic conflict constellation, while they may be profound, demonstrate a responsiveness to environmental change, being increased by some stimulus conditions, diminished by others. The total conflict pattern itself may become a relatively fixed part of the personality, but not so firmly fixed as the deficit patterns to be

described below. Conflict patterns, however intense, continue to reveal their association learning (conditioning) origins in their basic malleability, always remaining susceptible of some change in response to varying circumstances. Deficit patterns, on the other hand, resemble in their absolute immutability the behavioral effects of chronic organic lesions of the central nervous system.

2. Insofar as early life experience fails to provide opportunity for the exercise of certain capacities for sensory, motor, and cognitive-integrative functions and for the acquisition of certain secondary (noninnate) drives—i.e., insofar as the infant is deprived of the stimulus opportunities for such experience—there seem to develop patterns of deficit in related areas of behavioral function. Such deficit patterns differ from the patterns of fear-induced, conflict-mediated inhibition in that deficits are much more fixed and unresponsive to environmental change, resembling in this respect the behavioral deficits of hereditary or constitutional origin or those resulting from ablation or other irreversible loss of c.n.s. tissue. For human infants the period during which stimulus deprivation has its important deficit-producing effects seems to be roughly the first six months of life.

B. As Bowlby has implied in his brief reference to the stimulus deprivation concept, if there are two processes, they would usually both reach the infant through disturbed mother-child relationships. (Bowlby, 1969, p. 297; see the Reading Notes below). It follows that in many individual cases the two causal circumstances, emotional trauma and stimulus deprivation, will occur in the same infant. This need not always be the case, however. Though the crisis periods for the two processes appear to overlap, there is some time separation. It is possible therefore for an infant to avoid the major impact of stimulus deprivation in the first half-year but experience the traumatic effects of separation to a wide variety of events which may occur within or around the mother during the period after he has formed an attachment to her. The reverse is less likely, for epigenetic reasons. Once stimulus-deprived (and presumably then deficient in certain basic capacities), the infant in the second six months and beyond is unlikely to avoid evoking maternal rejection and consequent trauma. Thus, the period of vulnerability to stimulus deprivation may be considered an epigenetic stage one step earlier than the earliest described by Erikson. The same epigenetic considerations apply, of course, to miscarriages of genic and prenatal processes during what may be considered a still earlier crisis period, two steps removed from Erikson's oral-sensory (trust vs. mistrust) stage (see Fig. 11).

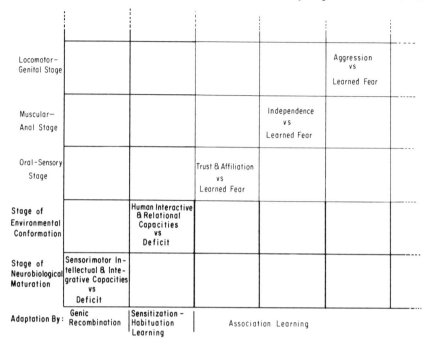

| | Adaptation By: | | | | |
|---|---|---|---|---|---|
| Locomotor–Genital Stage | | | | | Aggression<br>vs<br>Learned Fear |
| Muscular–Anal Stage | | | | Independence<br>vs<br>Learned Fear | |
| Oral-Sensory Stage | | | Trust & Affiliation<br>vs<br>Learned Fear | | |
| Stage of Environmental Conformation | | Human Interactive & Relational Capacities<br>vs<br>Deficit | | | |
| Stage of Neurobiological Maturation | Sensorimotor Intellectual & Integrative Capacities<br>vs<br>Deficit | | | | |
| Adaptation By: | Genic Recombination | Sensitization–Habituation Learning | Association Learning | | |

Figure 11. Proposed extension of Erikson's epigenetic schema by the addition of two earlier stages (see the text, chapter 12, I. A2, I.B, and III).

1. W. R. Thompson has recently suggested that the variable rates of differentiation of sensory and motor functions in the young animal may be an important determinant of the sequence of gene-environment interaction phases. – W. R. Thompson, "Development and the bio-physical bases of personality," in E. F. Borgatta and W. W. Lambert, eds., *Handbook of Personality Theory and Research* (Chicago: Rand McNally, 1968), pp. 149–214.

   a. In a first phase neither input nor output is significantly differentiated, and the only learning possible is that involving repeated general arousal or the evocation of some innate reflex. Such stimulation results, at a later time, in a difference in the animal's relatively general, undifferentiated responsiveness. Thompson concludes that "temperament" may be the behavioral area influenced by this early "habituation-sensitization" type of learning. The period involved includes the later portion of intrauterine life and the early postnatal period, the phase for which (in Fig. 11) the term "environmental confirmation" has been suggested.

**b.** In a second phase (Thompson uses the term "age-zone") input has differentiated significantly, but output remains undifferentiated. "Stimuli can be discriminated, but instrumental responding is still minimal" (p. 160). Classical conditioning and the acquisition of affective meaning are the learning processes characteristic of this period, which corresponds to the emphasis given above to the importance of the earliest Eriksonian conflicts for later emotional orientation.

**c.** During a third age-zone, both input and output are differentiated, a whole variety of responses is possible, and the characteristic learning is that of adaptational techniques through instrumental conditioning.

**II. Some studies of trauma and inhibition in infancy: early interpersonal conflict**

**A.** As has been stated previously, studies of the effects of loss following initial early attachment to the mother represent a more detailed look at Erikson's trust vs. mistrust period (or at its earlier component if one accepts his occasional leaning toward subdivision) and thus at the childhood interpersonal origins of trust-fear and some submission-fear conflicts. The literature in this area is voluminous. A few well-known clinical studies will be cited, and the Reading Notes provide suggestions for further study.

**1.** In 1946 Spitz and Wolf described the syndrome of "anaclitic depression" occurring in some infants who, *after the establishment of a good relationship with the mother*, were subjected to separation from her. Over a period of several months these infants showed the following sequence: increased irritability, demanding-ness and crying, screaming when approached, and withdrawal and loss of interest, with gradually increasing rigidity and frozenness of expression. The condition was relieved by return of the mother or replacement with a suitable and consistent substitute. — R. A. Spitz and K. M. Wolf. "Anaclitic depression," *Psychoanal. Stud. Child.* 2:313–42, 1946.

**2.** Very similar to the children whom Spitz and Wolf studied was the patient Monica, of Engel and Reichsman, whose mother could not "mother" her comfortably because the patient suffered from a congenital deformity. Both studies demonstrate the prominence of *withdrawal* in the behavior patterns induced by early trauma of this sort, as well as the intensity of the anxiety and the empty, despairing quality of the depressive affect. In addition, Monica points up the fact that total physical separation from the mother is not necessary; disturbance of the quality of the relationship, if great enough, can produce severe disturbances in the child. Monica also illustrates the frequent overlap in the same patient of deficit and conflict processes. The authors state: "It is our impression that on admission to the hospital Monica presented features reminiscent of both 'hospitalism' [i.e. deficit; see below] and 'anaclitic depression' [conflict]" (p. 440). – G. L. Engel and Franz Reichsman, "Spontaneous and experimentally induced depressions in an infant with a gastric fistula: a contribution to the problem of depression," *J. Am. Psychoanal. Assoc.* 4: 428–52, July 1956.

3. In an important 1960 paper John Bowlby summarized the 12-year findings of Robertson and Bowlby on children subjected to separation from the mother figure between the ages of 15 and 30 months. These children commonly show a syndrome very similar to those described above, characterized by phases of protest, despair, and detachment. – John Bowlby, "Separation anxiety," *Internat. J. Psychoanal.* 41: 89–113, March-June 1960.

4. Withdrawal (detachment) is not the only behavioral outcome which seems to be related to separation from adequate mothering in early life. Excessive, inappropriate, self-defeating *aggression* (often in the form of delinquency or antisocial behavior) is also apparently related to such experiences. In an earlier paper Bowlby described a pattern of "affectionless" personality in a large percentage of juvenile thieves. These children had suffered loss of relationship with the mother, and their behavior seemed to reflect determination "at all costs not to risk again the disappointment and the resulting rages and longings which wanting someone very much and not getting them involves." – John Bowlby, "Forty-four juvenile thieves: their characters and home-life," *Internat. J. Psychoanal.* 25: 19–53, 107–28, parts 1 and 2, 3 and 4, 1944.

## III. Some data on stimulus deprivation and deficit

A. Here again there is a very large literature, including many studies on various animal species. Some of the animal work will be summarized and two well-known studies cited. The reader is again referred to the Reading Notes for further study.

1. There is a large body of experimental work suggesting that in some species, deprivation of visual stimuli during postnatal life results in poor visual discrimination when such stimuli are first permitted. The deficit is not usually permanent. Experimenters have found evidence of actual organic damage (e.g., retinal and c.n.s. degeneration). Animals deprived in early postnatal life of the opportunity to peck or suck have failed to develop these behaviors when such opportunities are later given. The ability to learn seems to depend upon early opportunity to "practice learning" or, at least, to be exposed to a certain minimum level of perceptual experience in early life. In many species the absence of early contact with members of their own species permanently impairs the ability to engage in intraspecies reproductive activity. The effect here seems to be on the sensory side; i. e., members of the individual's own species do not evoke reproductive behavior. The reproductive behavior pattern itself is not essentially changed. Capacity for flocking and other "social" activity within certain species is frequently dependent upon contact with members of that species during an early and often narrow "critical period." The experiments on *imprinting* constitute the main body of research in this particular area.

   a. In some respects the processes by which deficits result from inadequate sensory stimulations seem to resemble imprinting, or more correctly, failure to imprint. Some workers prefer to limit the term "imprinting" to the phenomenon observed in some species of precocial birds in which the chick shows a marked perceptual preference for the object to which it has been exposed during a narrow critical period in its very early life. Furthermore, despite the characteristics of the critical period, rapidity of acquisition of the response, relative irreversibility, and other qualities which seem to differentiate imprinting from association learning (conditioning), there has recently been some doubt expressed whether the two learning processes are truly separate. Nevertheless, there does appear to be some useful analogy to be drawn between the effects of adequate sensory stimulation during the first six months of human life and imprinting, and between the effects of stimulus deprivation during this period and failure to imprint.

2. Harry Harlow has found that monkeys raised in complete social isolation from other monkeys for the first six months display in later life fixed and severe incapacity to integrate their behavior into any of the patterns of monkey social life: play, mutual grooming, sex, maternal activity. It is also true that these animals show re-

sponses of violent fear and aggression toward other monkeys. Thus the results again point up the difficulty of assigning even an animal experiment exclusively to the deficit category as opposed to the conflict category. — H. F. Harlow and M. K. Harlow, "Social deprivation in monkeys," *Scientific American* 207: 137–46, November 1962; and "The effect of rearing conditions on behavior," *Internat. J. Psychiat.* 1: 43–49, January 1965.

3. Studies of children placed in institutions at an early age reveal with considerable consistency impairment of general intellect, language function, and abstract thinking. R. Spitz in 1945 reported a study of foundling-home infants reared in an aseptic, physically adequate environment essentially devoid of opportunity for contact with people. These infants showed a marked retardation in all areas of psychological development (motor coordination, language, habit training, social activity), were very poorly developed physically, and were very susceptible to infections. There was an extremely high mortality rate among them. In a follow-up study after two years, there was still marked retardation in the surviving members of this group as compared with a control group of children in an institution but in good contact with their mothers. Spitz called the syndrome observed in these foundling home children "hospitalism." — R. A. Spitz, "Hospitalism: an inquiry into the genesis of psychiatric conditions in early childhood," *Psychoanal. Stud. Child* 1: 53–74, 1945.

a. Spitz makes no specific effort to relate this syndrome to the mental illnesses of adult life, but Bellak has proposed that some forms of the schizophrenic syndrome may represent the effects of such deprivation "in a period when the somatic development of the sensory and motor apparatus requires 'polarization' toward and by external stimuli of a consistent nature (mother figure)." — Leopold Bellak, "The schizophrenic syndrome," in L. Bellak, ed., *Schizophrenia: A Review of the Syndrome* (New York: Logos Press, 1958), pp. 3–63.

### Reading notes

The best general reference for this chapter is John Bowlby, *Attachment and Loss,* vol. 1, *Attachment* (New York: Basic Books, 1969). The second volume, dealing with loss, is still in preparation, but will no doubt review in great detail the issues of early emotional trauma and resulting conflict. Meanwhile see John

Bowlby, "Separation anxiety: a critical review of the literature," *J. Child Psychol. Psychiat.* 1: 251–69, February 1961; "Pathological mourning and childhood mourning," *J. Am. Psychoanal. Assoc.* 11: 500–541, July 1963.

The clearest argument for the importance of stimulus deprivation is made by Lawrence Casler, "Maternal deprivation: a critical review of the literature," *Monogr. Soc. Res. Child Develop.,* no. 80, vol. 26, pp. 1–64, 1961. The review of animal work on early experience from which the summary was prepared is F. A. Beach and Julian Jaynes, "Effects of early experience on the behavior of animals," *Psychol. Bull.* 51: 239–63, May 1954. More recent work, and a cautious appraisal of the general significance of imprinting, are presented by William Kessen, "Comparative personality development," in E. F. Borgatta and W. W. Lambert, eds., *Handbook of Personality Theory and Research* (Chicago: Rand McNally, 1968), pp. 365–410. Also useful on imprinting, and somewhat more enthusiastic about the implications for psychiatry, is E. H. Hess, "Ethology," in A. M. Freedman and H. I. Kaplan, eds., *Comprehensive Textbook of Psychiatry* (Baltimore: Williams & Wilkins, 1967), pp. 180–89.

# Index

# Index